What Clients Don't Tell Management Consultants -

What Consultants Should Do
What Clients Should Know

Y Kwan Loo

BSc(Eng) MBA CEng MIET MIMechE MCMI MCIM FRSA

authors
On Line

Visit us online at www.authorsonline.co.uk

An Authors OnLine Book

ISBN 978-07552-0438-0

Authors OnLine Ltd
19 The Cinques
Gamlingay, Sandy
Bedfordshire SG19 3NU
England

This book is also available in e-book format, details of which are available at www.authorsonline.co.uk

ACKNOWLEDGEMENTS

"I am eternally grateful to my long suffering wife and business partner Cheng for her ongoing support and company on this eventful roller coaster ride. Most importantly, many thanks to all my Clients and Associates who have kept K-L Associates going since 1989. My appreciation to Julian Roskams (Etica Press) for his editing and Richard Fitt (AuthorsOnLine) to make it all happen."

Y Kwan Loo
2008

Contents   Page

vi

Introduction

This unique book attempts to answer a number of interesting but important questions: -

What is life really like working as a full-time business management consultant?
    -    i.e. is this the right career for you?
Is consulting an easy option and full of glamour?
Are all prospects/clients the same and what types are there?
Do you find that marketing and selling of your services a real piece of cake or a tough act?
What responses would you expect to receive at various stages of client engagement?
What types of signals might you receive when prospecting for business (are females different)?
How do you know that your clients are really truthful – is that actually important?
Would you enjoy reading a consultant's interesting and real-life autobiography?
Are there cultural differences between a typical British and non British company?
What are the different needs and concerns of various clients?
Are there common strengths and weaknesses within firms?
What types of projects might be handled?
Now that you know about the ins and outs, will you *survive* and thrive in a consulting career?
Should clients treat consultants the same way as other service providers?
How should a prospective client behave to achieve a 'win-win' (mutually beneficial) outcome?
How can clients possibly shoot themselves in the foot?
What actually can a practising consultant do to succeed?
Are there tangible rewards as a practising consultant that you can talk to anyone about?

If you are already in business or aiming to be a successful entrepreneur, you will find some useful nuggets of information, interspersed with hard-won insights here. You may well discover that you have missed the boat that could have taken you to greater success and wealth for your business. For some of you, hopefully, it is not too late to rectify your situation and catch up.

I have used quite down-to-earth language and terms, which should be familiar to most business people. This book is intended to be informative, interesting, succinct and factual – all of these at the same time and definitely non-academic in style. Being candid and direct have always been my hallmark.

A little background about me will help. Since 1989 I have worked as a business management consultant, assisted by my handful of fellow associates. Professionally qualified as a Chartered Engineer with a blue chip company, my initial interest and focus lay with engineering, technical or scientific organisations. My unofficial 'patch' is the UK, targeting businesses that are predominantly located in the South-East of England. Since clients, especially prospects, have never offered to pay for my travelling expenses, this makes good financial sense.

This book describes my real-life experiences, drawn from direct contact with countless prospects and many clients. For obvious reasons, no genuine names are mentioned and those given are fictitious. However, I like dealing with facts and this is basically non-fiction. Hence the anecdotes mentioned are REAL, albeit influenced by my personal opinions. Thus, it is likely that some of you may even recognise yourselves in this book! Well done if you do, especially if your fortunes have expanded via my involvement. Some prospects will hopefully also realise that they should bear the blame for some of the 'lose-lose' outcomes where nobody has gained. To shield any client from being easily identified, some circumstantial details have been modified or omitted. I have enjoyed giving my time and efforts to most of my clients. To them, I would say 'thank you' for the pleasure.

A few clients have asked me why I have chosen to become a consultant. My answer is fairly straightforward. Having worked for years in a technical discipline and subsequently in management, one issue has always emerged as a personal bugbear. Companies are run by people, and the latter are by no means perfect due to our human limitations and frailties. My personal ambition is unencumbered by internal corporate constraints and politics, so I can freely speak my mind. Ideally, I have always wanted to be on par with those with the power to effect important changes. The only pragmatic way for this to happen is for me to be an independent consultant where there is no official 'boss' whom I have to please! It is now a case of not being able to enjoy repeat business if my client is dissatisfied.

Why should I invest my time and intellectual efforts in writing this book?

Although I aim to continue consulting into the foreseeable future, for as long as I can sustain and exploit my intellectual prowess, no one can really predict accurately. With my personal interest in health-related topics, I should fare better and, hopefully, last a bit longer than some.

It is therefore my intention to share my hard-earned knowledge, which I have gained over these 20 plus eventful years. Much of my story relates to thousands of cold calls, hundreds of meetings with prospects and the execution of many interesting and challenging projects.

For fellow veterans in this consulting game, you may well recognise similar events in your own lives and.....do smile please! For the budding consultant, I hope that this book will shed useful light for your future and prepare you for a fairly smooth ride, probably dotted with both ups and downs, i.e. the notorious 'feasts and famines'. Finally, only prospects and clients, who have behaved honestly and impeccably, should congratulate themselves! I do look forward to helping all of you further. New ones are welcome to join my long list. Happy reading everyone!

One thing is certain in this book, you will definitely discover much more than you have negotiated (or ideally paid?) for. If you are naturally shy of the 'truth', then this book is **_not_** for you.

Y Kwan Loo, BSc(Eng) MBA CEng MIMechE MIET MCIM MCMI FRSA
Principal
K-L Associates
Email: kwan@k-lassociates.com
Website: www.k-lassociates.com

Chapter 1   First Contacts With Clients

Unless your client comes naturally to you, you would normally have to initiate the first move to locate your client. Many well-known ways exist for successfully making initial contacts with prospects. We hope that they will eventually become our clients. 'Eventually' is a key word since the incubation period can literally run into many months and years - a real dilemma if you expect immediate financial results. The common or most used methods are through a mutual contact ('referral'), a direct mail shot, cold-calling by telephone, networking at events and meeting at unusual venues. Hitherto, I cannot remember obtaining a client as a direct result of advertising in printed material, i.e. directories, journals etc. A good proportion of consultants get their first assignment from their ex-employers. This may seem a real cop-out for the ambitious, but every client counts.

Personally, I found that all these can be productive but the end results can be somewhat unpredictable. I should add that I was fortunate enough to benefit from a very steep learning curve in selling my services, when I paid dearly membership from a new 'consulting' franchise. This happened at the very beginning of my consulting career. Sadly, this support survived for less than a year and had disappointed many who had joined with high hopes.

Cold calling

Over the years, I must have made close to 100k cold calls to 'strangers' (i.e. those whom I have not met face to face before I made the phone call). For me, it has become so natural to cold call that I have even been occasionally paid for to coach sales people using my well-honed techniques. Even with my well-weathered exposure, I am always amazed at what these prospects would say to me over the phone when they were first approached. Their reactions can vary greatly.

The most productive calls were those where an element of 'familiarity' was present. What I mean is that the calls were not 100% 'cold'. Examples were ones where I have been given some details, whose colleagues or friends I might know or with whom I had made some form of contact in the recent past. These would give me some 'excuse' to make contact and for the recipient to invest a few seconds. The recipient would be the crucial link in determining the next stage. You would normally have just one opportunity to make the correct and positive impact. Any signs of verbal incomprehension due to stuttering could mean total loss as far as that prospect is concerned.

I am pleased to say too that making cold calls has become an essential marketing/selling tool although it is not the only tool. I have never met a successful, self-employed or independent consultant who would never need to cold call. There are some consultants who would depend on others to obtain projects, surprisingly similar to 'biological' parasites. Given the choice, I would find it difficult to select that option knowing full well that there are opportunities out there waiting to be taken. However, I do accept the generally held view that cold calling is not necessarily the best method within the context of British culture. But it does have its place amongst all the other forms of selling. Sitting back, literally doing nothing and praying for potential clients to make contact, will be a definite recipe for failure for a small, unknown business.

With the recent legislation on constraints (i.e. those who cannot be 'cold called') affecting the telephoning of strangers, you will need to be a little more careful and be sensitive enough not to cause upset. Many companies expect to be called since that is an established and effective way of doing deals. You can certainly compare this with the style usually adopted by the US-based financial kids.

Cold calling does have several advantages. It can impart a positive image of confidence to most clients, if it is executed correctly. If you fail to project sufficient self-confidence, it is unlikely that you will succeed in selling. This will generally apply to most situations. It is also an exciting, and a challenging opportunity to demonstrate your mettle in the face of the unexpected. You must have the wits to think on your feet and respond appropriately! There is no doubt that it needs guts to do it really well.

Many would agree that cold calling is not a natural behavioural act that suits everyone, even including seasoned consultants. The skill and confidence required to cold call successfully are surprisingly uncommon among most people. If it is not for you, then a possible solution is to pay someone else to do it on your behalf. Various so-called telemarketing firms have sprung up to offer such a service. However, there are many disadvantages to using such help. The main ones are: -

- Loss of initial and potentially critical impact by not utilising your natural charisma (have you any?) and personality
- Loss of some continuity in the business relationship when you will, inevitably, need to take over at some time in future
- The costs of paying somebody (especially for non-tangible results) can soon mount up and may become prohibitive (i.e. how does £180 per appointment sound to you?)
- There is likely to be a negative reflection on you and your firm, by not projecting a strong or competent image that would be achieved by directly approaching your customers
- You will miss out the opportunity of personal learning and development from the process
- You will suffer incomplete knowledge of how the relationship has developed over time, thereby not benefiting from the 100% understanding of the client's issues

One annoying aspect of cold-calling is, invariably, the cost of making the phone call. Due to the highly competitive and now liberalised phone market, most geographic numbers should cost next to nothing to call. The 'best' ones are the cheapest, e.g. with the 0800 prefix. Those that cost more are the 0845s, followed by the very annoying and extortionate 0870s. When a firm uses a 0870 number, it will pocket quite a tidy sum from the callers (currently 9p per minute using my phone company). Normally, the excuse made by the subscriber is that a local rate is assumed to be charged. To me, it indicates greed in the users' attempts to extract every penny possible. By doing so, it might even hint at the existence of financial hardship or cultural meanness in that firm, which surely, cannot reflect well, image wise. Thus, you ought to be more aware when approaching these companies for business. But, will they be happy to part with their hard-earned pennies, currently made from their 0870 phone numbers? From experience in contacting such firms, I have detected some evidence of abnormal behaviour or sharp practices.

Networking

You may expect hits on your website but don't rely on that. You will need to seek out business yourself. Statistically speaking, it is impossible to know enough people within your networks and just to rely on their friendly referrals. There are literally thousands (if not millions) of potentially good prospects out there, waiting to be courted for their business. The more companies you make contact with, the more will become your clients. According to one well-known Chinese saying: 'If the East firm/family is unwelcoming/unproductive, go to the one in the West.'

Meet prospects in a variety of business and social situations. Some of these occasions can be a waste of time, especially when other more pushy consultants are blatantly plying their wares at the same event. This can be very off-putting to those prospects who have been victims of such approaches. In their minds, your prospects could be thinking 'Not another time wasting bl..dy consultant'. However, I am very spoilt for choice as to which social gatherings I should 'hunt' in since I am associated with several professional bodies.

You are probably aware of the recent marketing phenomenon, which expounds the usefulness of 'networking'. It often assumes that the crack of dawn, i.e. early breakfast, is the ideal time for networking events. Having attended a few such events, I have concluded that these are far from ideal to develop my own line of business.

The usual attendees tend to be sole practitioners, lone traders or owners of micro businesses, who would hardly need or can afford to pay much for advice. Many of them are there to offer fairly common goods or services such as legal advice, DIY, plumbing, electrics, IT, accounting, and gardening. For them, these events can be excellent, fertile grounds to exchange leads and sell to each other. What these business people expect is a forum in which to exchange business ideas and obtain useful solutions for free.

You can certainly network to build a large database of individuals with such common skills. However such a network needs much investment of time, efforts and nurturing to keep it active and productive. As expected, apart from the time element, there is a cost involved too, to be a member.

Another form of 'e' networking that involves online membership is becoming more widespread too. Depending on how deep your pockets are, they offer several grades of membership, including paying a fee as you physically participate. The basic level is normally free but it is highly restrictive as to what you might get in return. After all, we all have to 'eat' sometime, and lunch or dinner is definitely not free! The founders or organisers aim to provide the advantage of a limitless, virtual network so that there can be ongoing dialogue between members online or via frequent face-to-face events held in public venues, such as wine bars. Recently, I have been invited to apply to become a 'free', permanent life member. Again, such networks tend to attract mainly individuals or start-ups, where quite cheap or even free advice is eagerly sought from fellow members. The needs of such members are underdeveloped and their financial pockets are inevitably very shallow. From my observations, it seems fairly accurate to say that the main aim for networking is to *sell* one's products or services.

Some initial meetings

The conversion ratio from the very first meeting or contact into an agreed project can vary drastically. There is always the keen expectation that this meeting will result in an interesting contract. However, many factors can come into play here. Several examples are now described.

I met up with a managing director who ran a sign-designing business in the posh part of central London. Our interesting meeting touched on several personnel issues, particularly on the effectiveness of how he conducted his current appraisal system. It is well known that a high percentage of these systems frequently fail to achieve a high satisfaction level in practice. However, when I phoned him later, as agreed in our meeting, he would not talk to me.

When we met at a public event, a managing director of a filtration company enthusiastically agreed that we should meet. Both of us are fellow Chartered Engineers, and I thought to myself that perhaps I was in luck. But when I phoned him as agreed, soon after the event, he had since decided that there was nothing I could do for him as he was fairly happy with his sales, current technical director etc. Thus, a positive, initial contact does not necessarily guarantee a good outcome. Agreeing to talk or meet later can be an easy, positive way to end an interaction with someone who is trying to sell you something.

Similarly, a friendly CEO of a voice products company, which had a recent management buy-out, asked me to make contact. I did so as arranged, and his reply was for me to call again in a week's time if I did not hear from him. This was because he would be busy making appointments himself after the seminar. As predicted, he did not call me. Therefore, I contacted him again to hear that he had decided that it would not be the correct policy to use external services.

One case concerned a small firm involved in the maritime printing business. The MD was obviously keen but his second in command was not. They said that they would now be aware of how I could help but preferred to wait and see whether my help might be needed at some point later. With just 20 staff, this means that there would be limited scope to help them. The main outcome of this was a more senior contact I managed to make with within another group of companies, which happened to share the same site and industry sector in East London.

I was rather excited in anticipation when I cold-called a US subsidiary making electrical items. They had links to the famous Lucas brand. The new, fairly friendly European president agreed to meet me a few days later. He started by commenting that he did not know me (hence my purpose of the introduction). He had replaced much of the traditional and long-serving workforce with people he knew from the past and elsewhere. According to him, he could only go by what he termed as 'past performance'. Despite being there for only 4 short months, he had reorganised his slim management structure and embarked on an outsourcing strategy for this products. Apparently I was months too late but I was asked to wait a while to check the consequences of his actions.

England is famous for its craft-related and pottery industries. Apart from the few renowned and household names in Staffordshire, there are countless others operating on a smaller scale. At a public event, I met the sales director and managing director of one such small business, which employed less than 45 people. My subsequent meeting with the managing director seemed positive and there seemed a good chance of helping them with their management issues. In that meeting he told me that his company had just acquired another pottery business and that he was now preoccupied in assimilating the new assets. Sadly for me, this diversion of resources and doing nothing else meant that nothing could happen in the foreseeable future. It's really something for my backburner for the future but I am not optimistic as interest tends to wane as time passes.

My partner met someone at a publicly-run course she had attended. This led to several emails from me to this contact, a senior manager in a group of companies in food distribution. It emerged that cultural integration (of several acquisitions) was at the top of their agenda of current challenges. I was not surprised to hear that one of the big consultancies was already helping them in the areas of IT and strategy, apparently with varying degrees of success. This manager concluded that this state of uncertainty would make it difficult for my involvement at that stage. Probably this will be another tepid case, to be reviewed sometime in the far future.

My first client was the result of making one cold call telephone to the chairman running a company that dealt with film services in London. It seemed quite straightforward; the client was impressed by my work experience and qualifications, and by the expertise of my associates. His response on the phone was quite positive, an indication of at least some interest on his part. As the founder's son, he did not possess the essential know-how and leadership skills to grow his company, but he did like expensive toys (fast cars), pastimes etc. I am pleased to say that they are still in existence, albeit on a smaller scale after all these years, but under new management though.

Another interesting example concerned an older managing director of a large and successful plumbing-related business in London, who had a number of sons. He showed strong initial interest about tackling family succession, but he avoided my subsequent phone calls without giving any explanation. Perhaps he had found the perfect solution or more likely, his sons preferred to muddle on happily without any external intervention. This is what I would call the 'generation gap' factor, one that has lost me quite a few projects after an apparently good start. A few years later, I made contact with the managing director's grandson. The latter was happy to mention my existence to his father, one of the bosses in the family. Unfortunately, as a large, well-known company, they were already well served by other advisers. It is a case of joining the queue, I suspect.

One engineering firm based in Oxfordshire started by asking me to write in with my details. There followed four subsequent teleconferences with the managing director over a two-year period. The first three of those calls got a negative response. However, I was lucky on the fourth. The managing director lamented that the hi-tech industry was struggling. I replied saying that some companies had recovered after the recession, so why had his not? This ended with an appointment made with his personal assistant for a date two months later. However, the meeting ended with him saying that he would call me 'when the time comes'. Perhaps his pain level was still bearable then. However, he did ask me to approach one of his directors in regard to a marketing problem but it was apparently resolved in-house when their human resources director was involved.

Telephone responses to cold calling

Over the years, I have heard a wide range of phrases when I cold call. The list below gives a good representative sample but this is by no means exhaustive. For expediency, I have generally assumed that my prospects are men. First reactions and replies do vary enormously (mainly from receptionists and personal assistants): -

'Have you spoken to him before?' (To check if you are cold calling or are a total stranger, and hence may possibly upset his boss. This can be an intelligent check to keep out the timid caller.)

'He's very busy/tied up/involved with...' (Common approach to avoid contact because you, the caller, are unknown or perceived to be unimportant.)

'Does he expect your call?'	(Yes, he expects to be called, naturally; otherwise he should not be in business. Unless he prefers to be a hermit?)
'Haven't seen him yet'	(This is plausible since the receptionist may have come in later than my prospect or is located separately in another spot.)
'Not available'	(For what? It's another very common ploy used to put you off.)
'On the phone/conference call'	(*Everyone*, including the boss, has to sell something. He is probably expending efforts on customer-related issues.)
'In a meeting'	(A very, very common response, probably true most of the time. However, not all meetings are the same.)
'Gone out/abroad/travelling'	(Normally, this cannot be confirmed. When is he returning?)
'On holiday'	(Common reply in the summer months – possibly true.)

'Does not or won't speak to you'	(What have I done to offend him?)
'Won't take this type of call'	(Perhaps he is a shy kind of recluse.)
'Won't take unsolicited calls'	(Can you imagine that as a standard response to his own sales people?)
'Does not know you'	(That's why I would like to introduce myself, stupid! Doesn't he want to cultivate a wider network?)
'Never heard of him in this company'	(Probably he has left, was fired or an indication of his firm being disorganised but I could be wrong.)
'No longer works for the company'	(I would wonder, and might even ask, why? You must naturally ask who's the successor now.)
'He is not answering his phone'	(Why? Is there a personal assistant with whom I can talk?)
'Not at his desk'	(Possibly, it is the sign of a good, 'walkabout' boss or a late/busy one.)
'His PA is not in/not in yet'	(I don't really want to speak to his PA unless...)

'I'll put you through to his PA'	(I am not really that keen to talk to her, especially if she is a rottweiler and a tough 'gate keeper'.)
'Busy with a customer'	(Obviously he's doing the right thing and I am a lower priority for him.)
'Be in later'	(It is already 11 am; is he working late and when is he expected? A late call can be productive.)

'Very difficult to catch...leave him a message?'
(What message would you like me to leave? In most cases if I am seduced to leave one, it is a waste of time. I reckon that less than 10% of messages are acted on.)

'Best write in or email. I'll put it in front of him'
(The effort of writing is very likely to be wasted. But express some appreciation if the offer is genuine.)

'Leave your details and I'll ask him to call you'
(I will hear from less than 20% of such cases. So, should I patiently stay in, waiting and hoping that he would call? I might do so, only

if I have no alternative and this is a serious case.)

'What is it about, or what does it concern'
(Should I bother explaining? This is typical gate keeping in operation here. I may well need to explain carefully and convincingly.)

'He is not based here'
(May I ask where?)

'He has just walked in'
(This can be perfect timing if his office is located just a few steps away.)

'There is a board meeting today'
(This can be opportune too; i.e. later.)

'Would you like to speak to his PA?'
(No, not really, if I can help it; unless she is genuinely helpful.)

'I spoke to him but he is not interested'
(How does he know my objective and on what we can achieve together? Is he not interested in selling more? This may well be his loss if I could actually refer him a big, juicy sale or cure some of his company's major problems. Did s/he really

speak to him or was it a standard answer? I will probably never know.)

'Leave a message in his voicemail'

(Normally this is another waste of time but...)

'He would prefer to do it himself' (A potentially complex situation where a direct question would be needed.)

'He is busy...needs more information'

(I have already explained the purpose of my call.)

'Leave me your number and I'll ask him to call you'

(I very much doubt if he will do so.)

'It would be good if you would email him'

(What should I email him about? It would probably be deleted as junk; thus wasting my efforts.)

'He's very busy...got your email address..'

(Every boss worth his salt should be busy. An obvious case of little current or even future interest.)

Sometimes I am put through to the top man himself and without a hitch. The following are some of the replies that I hear.

'I prefer to do things myself...not interested in outside help...don't like cold calls/get many – we don't cold call in our business.'

(He is probably one of those rare control freaks who may not realise what he's missing, i.e. blinkered.)

'It is unlikely that we would use consultants now or in the future. Good luck.'

(An apparently honest answer, which is much appreciated and one that could save much time.)

'Can you do me a favour? Drop me a line and I will look at it and respond.'

(This could well have a positive outcome here but usually not.)

'We are already well served... but contact me in future... by all means.'

(A sincere answer with a tiny hint of potential interest. This is probably a no goer.)

'You are speaking to the wrong person.'

(Who should I approach then?)

'What do you specialise in....how can you help?'

(A careful answer is required here to hook him in!)

'I am very busy now... ring me......'

(You are currently classified as low priority that does not even deserve a few seconds on the phone now. There is no guarantee either that he will be around when you phone again at the prearranged time.)

'Do I know you?'

(An interesting and sarcastic question indeed. Probably not, since Kwan Loo is not Sir Richard Branson, is he?)

'No, I am not interested; now or in future'

(An honest, non evasive answer which I would always respect.)

Some real examples

It is worth bearing in mind that many of the above can be clearly, very obvious excuses for not talking to you, the caller. In some cases, the recipients are probably surprised by your calls. I have been told that some companies receive at least two calls a week from various management consultants. For these companies, I willingly offer them my sympathy for suffering from 'consultant fatigue'. On a few occasions, I have actually heard my prospect 'whispering' loudly to his receptionist or personal assistant, telling the latter what to say to me! I get a large number of sales calls too but I tend to be very honest in my responses. Time is a precious commodity. Unless you enjoy leading people up the proverbial garden path, I do not see any point in reacting evasively.

One so-called extreme case of my cold calling might be worth a mention here. I was targeting a Bosch subsidiary near London. As usual, the managing director, having mentioned his need to grow sales in a mature engineering market, then asked me to write in. Subsequent phone calls to him via his receptionist were unsuccessful in terms of reaching him or getting an answer. I was keen to get a response, irrespective of what the answer was, so that I could classify him for appropriate action. If he had categorically said 'no', I could sensibly ignore him forever. Having been told his phone extension, I persisted. Thus, one evening, his extension was answered but the phone was slammed down immediately after I had uttered my usual enthusiastic greeting! This happened three times in fairly quick succession. For the next 10 minutes, the phone was not picked up again. Eventually, the proverbial penny dropped – he *might* be consciously avoiding me then. But.....why? So, I tried again after 20 minutes. This time our English managing director answered the phone. In a highly irritated tone of voice, he said, 'Stop phoning me....please'. If only he had been honest and had said that earlier, he could have avoided being stressed unnecessarily. I have concluded that he did have at least a problem on his hands but I was probably not the chosen one to help him. Indeed, I would be keen to contact his successor and I shall be waiting.

Apart from having to be persistent and thick skinned, selling requires specific talent, empathy and skill (from training?). It is definitely not for the faint hearted, introverted and shy. Ideally it is also an activity which should not be embarked on continuously for long periods. You have to be really mentally alert and prepared in order to succeed in selling.

There are some individuals out there (thankfully, a minority) who are unnecessarily worried about divulging corporate information to strangers. Some prefer to give vague answers, such as just asking me to address my mail to the managing director (his name was not given) since they have a 'no name' policy. Or typically, they might ask, 'Why do you ask? What is this for?' Sometimes, the receptionist might say, 'I am not allowed to say.... I do not want him to be bombarded by....?' In such cases, I can use alternative contacts and means to find out what I need to know. I think that such people do have a genuine cause or two for being fearful or worried. For example, he may feel a threat to his job security. Perhaps his bosses might prefer to cultivate a climate of secrecy that inevitably engenders more stress lower down the hierarchy.

However, some of the receptionists and personal assistants I have spoken to have been courteous and helpful to me. They might suggest a good or better time to call back and have probably passed on the messages as agreed. In some cases, I have managed to become relatively friendly with them and they normally recognise my foreign sounding voice. As a result, they can be quite frank and tell me straight that their bosses are definitely not interested. They are in a better position to know about that than I am. There are many cases where their bosses have given a blanket instruction for them not to pass any strange calls through. They might prefer an easier life and not care about someone who could potentially disturb their status quo. However, they can't be guilty if their bosses have chosen to ignore the messages. An important question for bosses to answer is: How many good business opportunities do you think you might have lost since issuing your blockade instruction? Are you also aware that many successful companies rely on new ideas and external stimuli to be kept up to date and hence remain competitive? How would you feel if all the sales calls or approaches made by your own sales people were similarly rebuffed?

It is a fact that your enthusiasm tends to wane the longer you have worked for a particular employer. There is probably some truth in the phrase 'familiarity breeds contempt'. Keeping a high level of motivation and enthusiasm amongst the workforce seems to be a perennial management preoccupation for some companies. One outcome from this is that I do hear many home truths from the lower echelons of firms with which I have tried to make contact. Examples would include the more junior staff, receptionists, personal assistants and shop floor (blue collar) workers. This is another useful form of intelligence gathering about your prospects.

Many people will ask to be mailed or emailed with some information first, before entertaining a first meeting with me. Over the years, this method has yielded mixed results. Sometimes, their promises to make subsequent contact should be taken with a large pinch of salt. On many occasions, this request for information is a 'put off' ploy used by the prospects. They are probably not interested and are not upfront enough to say so. They might be curious as to who you might be. The proof lies in the subsequent number of people I meet. Approximately, only 30% or so agree to a subsequent meeting after I have written to them initially. There are a few reasons for this. You can only write so much in a letter unless a heavy tome of your 'specialisations' is expected. Too much content will dilute its impact. A brochure or leaflet is far too impersonal and unfocused to hook a sizable chunk of interest. However, the first impression made by a piece of hardcopy can be critical and its importance considerable. Sometimes an email is acceptable but I regard that as worse than a brochure as emails are now too commonplace even to evoke a little reaction. Another possible problem is that an email may not reach its destination. From a positive note, a written introduction may well be the only tiny opportunity available to get your foot in, behind the often heavily closed door! When similarly approached, I have asked for something in writing too, if there was an element of interest on my part. My justification is that I was keen enough not to miss out.

Personal assistants and their bosses' responses

Sometimes, a personal assistant might suggest sending in something in writing. In that case, only a very small percentage of their bosses (say 5%) are interested enough to meet. You must remember that it was the PA who had requested your note, not her boss. However, when I call back and speak to the boss, there can be many types of answers.

Examples of replies (with my corresponding thoughts) to all these requests for writing in are as follows.

'I have read your letter/email but there is no interest/need.'

(Another failure to hook his interest or is there a well-hidden reason?)

'I have not heard anything of interest'

(This can be like finding the proverbial needle – what would you like or expect to read?)

'I have not read (or digested) it yet...'

(My communication is just a page long. Where did you study? When will you read it? Will it ever be read? It only requires one simple decision.)

'I am not really interested'

(Couldn't he have said so in the first instance, thereby saving both of us time?)

'There is no work for you...'

(I'm not particularly looking for a full time job. Surely there must be something I can help you with?)

'This is a busy period...'

(Often an excuse and this can recur a few times, well into the months ahead. Who would frankly admit that they are *not* busy?)

'Up to my eyes in it'	(That's why I have called, offering to help him clear some of it to enable him to see better. If this recurs, this is normally a disguised 'No'.)
'I will call you when...'	(A prospect is very unlikely to call you, the seller. This is just a polite and civil answer, asking to be left alone and not be bothered. You will just be a blurred memory when that time comes.)
'I will call you later....'	(Another promise, which is unlikely to be fulfilled – less than 20% would do so as he becomes encumbered etc.)
'What was it about?'	(It is either a clear case of poor short-term memory or that I have made virtually zero initial impact some time ago. This means I will need to rewind back to square one, and then repeat my spiel. Perhaps, I can offer to send him another letter or email if he has a visual preference.)
'I have passed your letter to...'	(This, as expected, would seldom lead to anything; an apparent

kindly act of buck passing and probably wasting my time.)

'Give me a call on...'   (This can often result in a meeting and possibly, a project. But, it can also lead to disappointments if he subsequently changes his mind or conveniently forgets to be available for your call.)

'I am not allowed to use external...' (Even for a small project? How about your other, similar external 'experts' – auditors, lawyers, attorneys, translators, gardeners, cleaners etc....?)

'Talk to my PA to fix a date'   (Can be really sweet music to my ears but this is only the first step; the meeting might never materialise for months, especially if there are several subsequent postponements due to various diversions.)

'It is the wrong time/not a good time'
                                (This is probably a truthful response because of their situations, which I obviously can't see from my end. Is he thinking/planning his

departure for greener pastures? For some, there never seems to be a good time anyway.)

'It will be a waste of our time to meet
(Why? Are you 'perfect' then? Keeping your mind open for once could well be the best action. On many occasions, this has indeed wasted time.)

'Please speak to my director......' (Why? Is the buck being passed again, I wonder?)

'We don't use consultants.......' (Why? They might well have had a bad experience or he may know better himself? I can always rename my job title to suit.)

'Not worth calling us...try others' (An honest reply, which I do appreciate and *may* deserve some respect. It can be illuminating to know why, if possible.)

'Since our conversation, I have now got consultants helping me'
(At least I might have done him a favour by stimulating his initial interest but can still wish him luck. One particular managing director, who responded as such, was described as a 'nasty

piece of work' by an associate. Are his consultants likely to be boot lickers?)

One peculiar sort of case related to a good sized engineering company in Leighton Buzzard. My target was its site/finance director. The kind receptionist must have connected me to his extension for more than ten times but he would always seem to have perpetually switched on his voice mail, presumably to filter all calls. Eventually I managed to find out his mobile number, which I naturally used. Calling someone on his mobile often creates an urgent emphasis. Somewhat surprised that I knew his number, he asked me to write in, and I did. Subsequently, he had forgotten his request and asked me to leave messages with the receptionist, which I did too. Of course or as expected, he did not respond. Eventually, I did call him on his mobile again to check. He did sound annoyed this time and complained that this number was 'private' and asked my information to be left with his PA. Surprise, surprise, did he have a PA? Unfortunately, no, according to the receptionist! Would I waste any more of my time, stationery and postage stamp on him again? Not on your Nellie, my friend! If he was an ops director, maybe I would. But definitely not for a finance guy, who would presumably only focus on the pennies and very little else. To be accurate, I can literally count on both my hands finance people who have decided to become my clients on their own volition. This might seem typical stereotyping but actual experiences cannot be ignored.

The above clearly shows that making initial contacts is never easy. What is ever easy? It is probably the hardest stage or action to achieve in consulting. This is probably the main reason why many competent and apparently knowledgeable consultants have failed so miserably. They would normally have rejoined full time corporate life, sometimes camouflaged as an expert 'change agent'. As there is probably more supply (of consulting expertise) than demand via projects, it is a highly competitive professional services sector. Many people, including ex senior managers and directors simply assume that their experience automatically makes them perfect consultants. Many of these, sadly, face the truth of how tough it can really be in practice. This invariably means giving up and returning to full time employment when their situations do not improve enough to make it viable or when a full time opportunity is dangled in front of them.

The more calls or attempts you make, the more fruitful the results you can hope to achieve. Basic statistics (i.e. probability), you may well say. Unless you are extremely lucky, you sometimes need to make many calls to secure an appointment. There are days when I have made over 50 phone calls to numerous organisations without making an appointment. Occasionally, I might be able to fix three appointments from just making around 10 phone calls. To illustrate a point, a Lamberhurst associate wrote to over 100 medium- and large-sized firms in the Midlands region in England. His reward was just a tiny piece of work and a handful of potential contacts for the future. Whenever I mention the word 'timewasters', my wife and business partner, Cheng, often remark that I should move on and ignore these prospects. She has already remarked that trying something else, i.e. outside consulting, might well be a good option. My father often quotes a Chinese saying: 'Every piece of ginger is hot'. I will say more about the 'timewasters' and their kin in Chapter 4.

The most productive contacts are those made directly with people, who have been referred to me by clients or other close contacts. You may call them 'warmer' prospects as compared to those I might contact out of the blue. This might sound like stating the obvious to the so-called converted. Basically, my known contacts might have already literally 'sold' me well on my behalf before I approach their referrals. Thus my main task is to ensure the establishment of good initial rapport and an exact understanding of the client's needs before proceeding to the next stage. Alas, things must never be taken for granted in this game. The unexpected can always occur and even these contacts can result in nothing.

As one veteran has advised me, 'it is not over till the cheque has cleared into your account.'

A good example of the above relates to a client, who has already spent a tidy 5-figure sum invested in my services. Apparently, his Glaswegian managing director would be interested in my services too. From earlier telecons, I have already heard and hence am made aware of this managing director's objectives. My first face-to-face meeting with him would certainly prove interesting and decisive. It turned out that he was then well served by a long-term supplier of competitive services, whose strategy clearly relied on offering 'cut-price' or subsidised services. This might be expected in Scotland, where the proverbial penny could be difficult to earn. Things do seem markedly cheaper up there when compared with London. The challenge for me would be to somehow outshine this competitor of mine. This could prove rather tough since, for a start, I am physically located several hundred miles away. Apart from other issues, my client would have to foot my air fares and hotel bills. But this story did have a rather satisfying and productive ending, when I gained him as another satisfied client many moons later.

Postponed meetings

I have experienced postponed meetings many times over the years. You normally start with a list of targets to contact. There is usually some preparation or work to be done before these people are approached. For obvious reasons, my choice approach is by phone. On my lucky days, I manage to speak to my prospect on my first call. More often than I would prefer, and naturally hate to admit, I might have to make up to 20 phone calls, over a period of weeks, before I manage to speak to my 'man', the target.

Having caught my man, my main objective is a personal introduction, hoping to excite him into becoming my client, eventually. Hence appointments are normally made for this purpose. About 70% of my appointments take place as planned – the venue, date and time. This figure used to be nearer 85%, a decade or so ago. Hence, I am often the victim of a postponed meeting, which is naturally far better than one that is permanently cancelled. The latter are quite rare and probably amount to less than 10% of all my appointments.

Reasons given for postponing appointments can prove interesting reading. Some of the reasons given have been:-

'I am called away (or wanted) for another (more important) meeting or problem.'
'I (or PA) have double booked.'
'A client has suddenly decided to visit us.'
'I have another meeting at the same time.'
'He is still abroad on business.'
'He has gone off sick.'
'It would not be worthwhile to meet yet.'
'We have had some changes which need to be sorted out first before it will be worthwhile for us to meet.'
'There has been some misunderstanding about why we should meet, and hence it seems there is no point in meeting.'
'It is now not a good time to meet. Call me again.....'
'He is not here; his wife has just given birth.'

As evident from the above, you may not always be a high priority in most instances. You can sometimes detect the seriousness of the prospect's situation by the length of elapsed time between making the contact and appointment. At times, you might be accorded the respect of a low level door-to-door sales person and be treated like one!

There have been a few occasions when appointments made with my targets have been subsequently cancelled. It is imperative to use your energy and persuasiveness to obtain the all-important appointment. Without the face-to-face appointment, nothing can happen. However, obviously using force to create an appointment can easily rebound, as this is only the first step in the sales process where a good relationship and rapport are essential.

One occasion concerned a managing director of a fairly large consultancy/training company who was persuaded to meet me. This was achieved after a few 'cold calls'. Subsequently, I was emailed informing me the futility of our proposed meeting. On reflection, their organisation was over 300 strong in employee terms, far outmatching mine. However, I can assume that even they could benefit from some impartial external inputs. To gain entry and be able to help such an organisation would indeed be a great success.

Another case concerned a health care type company, which utilises a network of doctors in its business. I met its managing director at a rail engineering trade show. He was obviously totally committed and even appeared quite pressurised through his frantic mannerisms to acquire more customers. I made contact again subsequently, asking to meet him under calmer circumstances to explore possibilities. At first, he informed me that he had a sales consultant currently helping him. He finally agreed to meet me upon hearing of my potentially useful contacts in the rail industry within my network of associates. I was asked to email him details of the proposed meeting. A few hours later, he emailed me, informing me of his decision to cancel the meeting. Apparently he had looked at my website, which might have reminded him of his own business contacts etc. His main message was 'Consequently I believe that we would be wasting each other's time if we were to meet'. Like most professionals, I replied, saying that I did have genuine contacts that he could probably find useful. He had obviously made some assumptions and some of which might well be wrong.

An outstanding example concerned an industrial chemicals producer based in East London whose managing director postponed appointments with me three times. On the second occasion, he apologised and 'promised' that the third date would happen. However, one of his staff phoned up the day before our third date, apologising for having to cancel again, and asked me to contact his boss in six months, since the latter was rather busy. Was it a case of not being there or plain cowardice, I wonder? I also wonder how he might feel if he was at the receiving end of countless postponements? This managing director happened to be in his new role, as his father (the previous managing director) had died shortly before. I had a mixed (partially negative) impression of the father, whom I had met, and perhaps the current managing director was a chip of the old block.

Finally, the winner for giving me the shortest notice must go to a small construction firm operating from NW London. Its office manageress rang my office 30 minutes before the appointed time. Can you guess where I was at that time? Yes, I was sitting in my car on a public road (its car park was minuscule and its surrounding area was clamp prone), less than 30 yards from this company's front door. A subsequent 'pencilled' in executive meeting was also cancelled without her notifying me. Earlier on, its managing director had kept me waiting for more than 30 minutes whilst I was in its reception area. Nevertheless, I AM still hopeful that......

Chapter 2   First Meetings and Impressions

Invariably, the first meetings can be full of surprises; both joyous ones and big disappointments included. In my 20+ years, I must have made over 600 initial appointments to introduce myself. In the early years, a few butterflies have kept me good company in my stomach. Nowadays, it feels more like looking forward to acquiring an acquaintance, possibly a new friend, and embarking on something exciting and fresh within someone's organisation. This could be making a foray into the unknown, making an unusual discovery within the realms of varied human behaviour. It is also interesting to note that some of my prospects would show obvious signs of apprehension in meeting me – something which I have to be conscious of. Presumably, seeing someone in the flesh is very different from just hearing a voice, particularly in my case, with my Malaysian Chinese accent. The one main conclusion is that you can never be 100% certain how the first meeting will turn out.

One thing is fairly certain: it is vital to be punctual for meetings. On the handful of occasions when I have been late, the results had been, regrettably, negative. Reasons for my lateness were mainly unexpected heavy traffic, delays caused by road accidents and having lost valuable time in locating the offices. There is usually nothing worse than appearing flustered when you are trying to make a positive impression. The same should apply to all my meetings with my clients when I am executing a project. Fortunately, I cannot remember being late for any of these meetings.

As expected, the majority of my initial meetings have resulted in 'nothing'. I can only vaguely remember being successful in fully agreeing to a piece of work on a few occasions at the first meeting. Probably, quite a bit of good luck was involved in those cases having a successful outcome.

Conversions and outcomes

My conversion ratio (from appointments to agreed projects) can vary widely from 1 in 1 to 1 in 12. An associate has observed over many years that only about 10% of initial meetings would result in a project. I should explain that most of these meetings were set up as purely exploratory and as unique opportunities to interest potential clients to proceed further. Demanding commitment to buy before any meeting has occurred could be counterproductive and it is not my style. It would seem impossible to strike a deal over the phone if both parties are uncertain of each others' situations and contractual obligations. Generally speaking, consumers of consultancy are a sophisticated breed of people, and it is important not to assume that they will give you their business.

Most prospects regard me as a relatively unknown quantity unless we happen to have something in common, such as being fellow members of a professional body. From years of exposure to a variety of situations, I can normally sense fairly accurately how these meetings will develop and what they may lead to. There are many occasions when the prospects' body language projects conclusive signals. In positive cases, I am either invited back to discuss things further or am virtually offered a contract on the spot. Other cases just form part of my long list of 'learning' experiences.

However, there can be unexpected negative outcomes as a result of resistance because of misconceptions or objections. In many cases, it is because other people, such as stakeholders within those firms, object. This can be the case even if my first contact was suitably impressed by my introduction. On the whole, few normal people happily welcome changes of any sort that could cause upset to their established way of life. The boss should realise deep within himself whether he needs to face the inevitable and bite the relevant bullet(s).

On a few occasions, I have suffered 'reverse' selling: prospects enthusiastically would talk about their own company and its products, hoping to make a sale themselves. This is generally time wasted. My main objective is to help them with their problems and be paid for it. I doubt if I have ever consciously introduced a subsequent sale to any of these companies. If these companies are already my clients, I would not hesitate to provide the bridge for their benefits. If it is I who take the initiative in the first place and have made the approach, I should be the one doing the selling and not be sold to by the other party. So, if you are guilty of this practice, do try to keep this to a minimum – it can only be to your advantage. If they have become my clients, then the story is very different, since further opportunities for my paid help may emerge through such interactions.

One excellent illustration was my meeting with a training manager of a large, well-known, London based security company. In the 35 minutes he allocated to our meeting, he talked about many issues, probably best summed up as follows:

> The fit between various components within the structure of this company
> Health and safety issues forming part of his job
> His company's primary objectives
> Ranking of his company worldwide and capitalisation
> Distribution of workforce and their locations worldwide
> The hierarchy and its heads of functions and departments, and where he fitted in
> Locations of various businesses, their sizes and directors involved
> Types of human resources tools and psychometric instruments used
> His own department, his team, roles of individuals and their various foci
> HR policies as regards manpower planning, methodologies used to solve problems
> Performance targets for each business sector etc, etc.

He rambled on non-stop well beyond my allocated time, without indicating any need for help! If that meeting was a good representation of what went on in his company, much time must have been wasted throughout. It was a case of over communicating the wrong type of information. Possibly, he was just acting out his usual role of trying very hard to convince others of his own worth in his company. Or, was he trying to fill up the meeting time, leaving me with hardly any time to explain what I could do for him?

Another type of meeting that seems a waste of time is one in which not a single important need seems to exist and I am there, apparently, out of the prospect's courtesy or usual curiosity about me. For example, one chairman ran a heart equipment company with around 30 staff. Apparently, everyone worked as a team. If a problem did emerge, they would get together to sort it out. Everyone was left to get on since they clearly knew what was expected of them. When I heard 'There has never been a problem', I could have made a quick exit through their front door then! His company had always gone forward. Even in the recession, they had managed to fight through and emerged unscathed. 'Any weakness at all?' I asked. 'Not aware of any' was his expected reply, and they were of the right size too. I was told that his management style was to be very kind, listen well and basically be fair. They had very few customer (mainly from hospitals) complaints. Staff attitudes were good and so was its organisational morale. Apparently, hardly anyone had left the company. So, was there any real concern at all? Well, possibly to increase sales as there was no problem with finance in the short term. Perhaps someone might need to be trained to succeed him as his right hand person? No, not really since there was apparently no time to do any of that.

Very few managing directors nowadays would spend more than two hours pouring out their thoughts etc. to a total stranger. They all know that time is money In a very primitive sense. However, I met an incredibly long-winded and patient managing director in the early 1990s who was involved in designing and manufacturing display cards. He started off by claiming to have an 'open enough mind', hence his agreement to meet me for an initial exploration. As chief executive of six companies, he had been through various organisational developments – fine, accepted. His preferred style tended to be involvement with all his management staff. He was pleased with most aspects but observed that everybody could be improved. They got their act together in operations, concentrating on BS5750 (a British Standard) and building on that under his 'very good' operations manager. He had the 'best' staff in manufacturing and they were also good with computers. The latter had cost him much money but he needed to replace his old 'wrong' computer. Hence estimations were now computerised and were in colour. Profit was very good in manufacturing. Not surprisingly, he labelled himself as the 'production man/ops director'. Sales-wise, they had a very short order book, reacting to needs and tended to be rather heavy with certain customers. A low percentage of his operations was product based and highly customised. He then commented that he had been there for 20 years, and hence implied being quite knowledgeable about the business! There were two divisions, with the turnover shared equally. It was becoming more diverse, becoming more established now and had succeeded in broadening the order book, with a maximum of 10% of total turnover per customer.

In the print division, there were still one or two large customers. One customer took 28% of the collective total, hence he felt highly vulnerable there. He was not sure about his strategies there. They had a monthly board meeting and the management team was regarded as very close. He was divorced from day to day operations till 2 years ago when everyone else was functional, including the chairman. The chairman was in charge of transport, delivery (with just four or five vehicles); the majority went through external carriers. Structure-wise, his financial director belonged to the group, assisted by a personal assistant. He was also the chairman and group sales/marketing director. He had two production directors, one managing the print side but officially not on the board. His two sales directors (none on the print side) were involved with customers and controlled the order book. This was because the print side ran itself! His production manager was equivalent to a divisional manager, being responsible for the sales team, consisting of one sales rep and 3 sales coordinators. The division manager did management work and ran the shop floor. The admin side of things involved the telephone, paperwork and managing the distribution list. He was left with the print side, which was more reactive than pro-active. The peaks were rather difficult to control or be timed. He meant that it was difficult to bring in the right work.

He concluded that he must have a plan or strategy, wanting no 'listless chickens' anywhere and admitting that 'external perspectives' were important. By the way, his ex-production manager was ex-ICL. To him, it was important for people to know the culture first. To sum up, all could be improved but the main problem was internal attitudes. He wanted to reduce vulnerability and increase machine utilisation. Although he was critical of solicitors' fees (quoted me the partner rate of £150 per hour), he was quite open-minded on a budget for my project. He deemed accountants and solicitors expensive as they were fee based. His main task was to evaluate initially. There was a need to convince him first, as being of great value was important to him.

Equally important to him was commitment. To him, no one could help him strategically and he had nothing specific on his mind. We concluded that he would send me an info pack. I returned to present a proposal to him but, as you might have guessed, nothing positive came of it! Although it was disappointing business-wise, this meeting was a great learning experience for me. However, when I returned to discuss my proposal with his fellow director, he admitted that there were real problems but that he had no great expectations and was not sure he knew the answer. As expected, like in the earlier meeting, he digressed into his thoughts and plans for investment but did admit that it would be worse if nothing were done. I could have saved several days by not doing the proposal and not returning to see him. The critical issue of timing arose, as regards Xmas etc.

In retrospect, the few buying signals were rather weak or hazy, and it was indeed a testing exercise on my patience and listening skills. You might well feel the same, having read my long narrative. It was probably a good example of someone who was too diplomatic (nice?) and hence not assertive or frank enough to tell me his rather low level of interest in the first place. Fortunately, since then, I have always consciously moved on if I feel that a meeting would be another waste of time.

Other types of prospects

Without boring you further, many first meetings entail listening to people pouring their hearts out. It may be a form of catharsis or relief, as observed by a young CEO. I would be at the receiving end when the prospects would describe their plans and future investments, strategies, relationships with their bosses and peers, changes within their HQ, their policies with consultants, their achievements to date, current products and services etc.

A good point that has come from such encounters is the amount of corporate knowledge that I have accumulated for possible future use. I cannot even contemplate how much such information I have gathered over the years but I might be unable to recall these consciously. One positive outcome must be a good boost to my personal self-confidence when I meet my new prospects. Hearing the same old stories might well make you feel rather blasé though.

On one occasion, a very personable owner and elderly chairman of an engineering firm digressed into telling me about the book he had written and had privately printed. The subject concerned a specialised form of machinery. He even gave me a free copy to take away. In the end, his 'modern educated' sons were not interested in entertaining outside help and wished to continue going their own merry way.

In 1997, I met the managing director of a medical company based just outside London. He gave me only half and hour, which he used for describing his company. Rather different from the manager in the previous paragraph, he gave full details of his organisational structure, six foreign offices, four business areas, throwing in all the directors' names, products for each area, numbers of people and turnovers in each country and the functions of each product. That was not the end! He went on to tell me about his future plans too. He was one of the few who wished to be addressed in the traditional manner, as 'Mr....', expressing his clear dislike for the American way.

The CEO of a telecom company explained that his chairman gave him 'intelligent advice'. With a company of more than 550 employees, he thought that his group was very strong and many of his employees had up to 20 years' experience. Since he would hire the best and also paid 'loads of money', there was no need to train anyone. His people would come to him already trained (possibly some by his competitors) and hence were experienced. The main message lay in his outstanding comment: 'we don't need consultants...they're no good at BT... (i.e. part of his company name, not the famous telecoms organisation)'.

There had been times when the need had not been immediate although I could have been potentially useful in one or more areas. Normally, this would mean making contact again to check after a number of weeks, months or even years! My record must be meeting someone again after 14 years! After this time interval, the chances are that prospects will have resolved their issues internally and my knowledge will definitely be obsolete. This prospect might be unable to recall even one fact about me. Unfortunately, it is likely that one of my many competitors will have sneaked in and won the prized project.

A good example of this relates to a project manager of a construction company whom I met via a fellow MBA. As an internal consultant, this manager had found life difficult as a 'change' manager. He had to endure internal politics and remain effective. If you were this person, it would be almost impossible to tell your own boss the truth, wouldn't it? If you could, there would be less need for consultants to relay the bad news.

For a long time, I was not thinking well and fast enough on my feet. Fortunately, as a result of a recent health related personal discovery, I have improved tremendously on my mental alertness.

One interesting meeting stood out from the rest. I spoke to a Chief Executive of a large hi-tech company, based along the M4 corridor, when he was abroad in the Middle East. Without any hesitation, he asked me to make an appointment to see him sometime via his PA. For a moment, I thought that this might well lead to a nice big project. As expected, I turned up on time as usual (I have probably been late in only 5% of my appointments). He appeared rather surprised – he had clearly mistaken me for someone else who might have shared a similar sounding name or company name! Sad to say, he just went through the motions, trying to be as courteous as possible and assumed a neutral body language.

Post meetings afterthoughts

For various fundamental reasons, some companies under-perform in several areas. The normal but serious consequences can be poor morale, low profitability, serious internal conflicts, extreme working stress/pressures etc. On a poor day, when I was not 100% alert, opportunities could quite easily slip through my hands. Some nationalities are inclined to drop hints or give certain body signals. On your own, it can be relatively easy to miss these split-second 'buying' signals or fleeting events. Having to listen quickly to the words, understand them, then respond or react, ask and make notes effectively at the same time is definitely a very tall order. Who is guilty of generalising that men are poor at multitasking? Sometimes, I was given the appointment because the other parties were somewhat curious about my offerings and also about me. It is also extremely easy to be wise after the meetings with the following thoughts:

Why didn't I ask him to clarify or to give more details relating to his situation?
Why did he grimace when he said that?
Was it something I said that caused him to give that negative signal or reaction?
Have I struck a raw nerve or made a real booboo?
Was he bored with my spiel, which might have stretched on just a wee bit?
Perhaps I should have probed deeper into his mess.
Why did he say that?
Why did he ask me that?
Was he subtly testing me; and in which aspects?
Have I lost control of the conversation?
Did I 'over' tell him certain information, thus inducing an undesirable negative reaction?
Was there any real chemistry (essential ingredient for any relationship) between us?
Were there any buying signals, especially subtle hints, which I might have missed?
Did he drop enough strong hints as to what I could do to help him?
Was I thinking fast enough on my feet or have I wandered off unconsciously into the oblivious, indulging in some momentary daydreaming instead?
Should I have been more assertive and closed the deal then?
Did I miss out something vital (defective listening skill) that was said or hinted at?
Should I have met somebody else in the organisation?
Was it psychologically or circumstantially a bad day to meet?
Did he treat the meeting with him as a free session to enable his catharsis?
Did I manage to convince him to buy?
What were his obvious objections (if any) and did I notice these?

Have I handled his 'objections' ineffectively?
Was there a hint that he would prefer sticking to his current consultants?
Did he make more than the normal amount of notes (possibly for future use as an internal consultant himself) or as a 'learning' opportunity for himself?
Was he obviously totally uninterested at all, normally deduced from his body language?
Should I have been more direct in offering the options?
Did I utilise my time wisely and motivate him well, making progress towards getting a sale on the spot?

Those who wasted my efforts

Let me tell you about some of my many disappointments first. There have been a small percentage of prospects, who had agreed to see me but who have somehow disappeared when I turned up at the appointed time. One managing director of a small engineering company in Uxbridge (by the canal, and it had a French-sounding name) appeared more than 30 minutes late, and he did look surprised that I was still around when he returned. From his manner, I could sense that it would be a wasted morning. Indeed, it turned out to be a wasted two days when my proposal fell on deaf ears at our second meeting. His assistant blatantly took it as an opportunity to learn how to sell by making copious notes of my presentation! I would never contact that company again and I have learnt a lesson or two from that experience.

In a few cases, PAs have had to apologise on their bosses' behalf when the latter have been absent. Sometimes, I could sense real embarrassment in those PAs' faces. I have now decided to set limits as to the number of times when a prospect can cancel the first meeting. It is the only way to preserve my sanity and be more productive with my efforts. On a number of occasions, someone has called me to cancel the meeting, incredibly, with less than an hour to go! This is a good indication of how these people actually manage, and thus, they could possibly be good targets to home in on. If there is a problem, there may well be a need. But it is also plausible that the level of interest is non-existent and that I should move on *pronto* to greener pastures.

There have been times when my original targeted prospect has referred me to see someone else within his organisation. The latter could be the HR director, personnel manager or a functional manager or head. In many of these cases, the meetings with these people have turned out to be a complete waste of time. First, these second-tiered persons I was asked subsequently to meet could only see a narrower, functional perspective, when compared to the top man's. Also, not having the power to decide and influence, this could mean limited ambitions or scope for them to achieve for their companies. To admit personal weaknesses or underperformance to their superiors could obviously spell disaster in certain cultures and generally would not look good. Also, how many subordinates would have the guts to reveal all to a total stranger unless they had strong initial interest? This might be especially true of a sales director, whose attitude is expected to be perpetually positive and who is expected to appear highly motivated. The only exception are cases when the managing director has already met me and would like another opinion from his right hand person.

From my observations, weak managing directors are normally ineffective leaders. Again, how many of these would be brave enough to admit that very clearly to their staff, let alone to external strangers? They might be charged with running failing, underperforming companies or even be guilty of mediocrity. Paradoxically, they might not realise that they, as managing directors should seek urgent help before it is too late even for them and their companies. But, the interesting question is – how did they get to their senior positions in the first place?

Persistence pays!

Persistence has been noted by many as one of my obvious, positive personality traits. Depending on my mood and instinct, I do persist on many occasions. My partner has naturally observed that too. One example concerns a technical consultancy comprising a number of specialist divisions. I had met the managing director at a public event and he had agreed that I should speak to his other directors too. His chairman was frustrated by their stagnant revenue stream and fluctuating profitability, which was attributed to low entry hurdles for competitors. There was a high percentage of repeat business. Their perennial problem revolved round the attraction and retention of key specialist staff. The layer of junior staff had suffered high labour turnover because of perceived, poor financial and career prospects. As the chairman and the biggest shareholder, he felt that he was not autocratic enough. He had observed that his managing director had not played his full part yet as the latter had not found the right staff to delegate properly. Even though they had a business plan, the focus had to be clearer, concentrating on implementation, especially sales and marketing issues. Another director felt that their client base was too small. Despite a constantly changing market place, things were not adapted to move things forward. Internal inefficiencies, lack of time and the low job rates paid were seen as the main obstacles. The tendency to 'pepper pot' things from widespread advice meant that there was fairly bad focus. Their clients had complained about the technical results, which might be perceived differently, internally, due to weak messages. Due to relatively poor pay, the non-graduate staff now had less enthusiasm for work. A combination of being relatively near to expensive central London and low profitability had meant that they could not pay as much; hence a vicious circle had ensued. Communication within divisions was good but not so between certain individuals. The director in charge of marketing and operational matters admitted that he did not enjoy making new contacts, as part of marketing. Cash flow was affected by late payments and bad debts. Interestingly, he said that due to time and cost he had not got round to doing more in marketing. The final director observed that their client base was not well connected and marketing was not meeting the right people. Their pricing policies were decided on an ad hoc basis. The overhead was fixed at around 40% and there was not the right backup staff in his division. These were all interesting comments, which, when combined, could present serious issues. The good news was that this company has finally become one of my recent clients. This happened about two years after my initial contact. It was a good job that I persisted on this occasion.

It was the second site leader that I saw in this multinational electronics company just outside north London. The first one had left, probably due to frustration of the internal reorganisations. The second saw that there was a weak design manager who might benefit from some personal development. Potentially, the skills set in its company production section might need to be more assembly focused. Neither needs materialised into a project due to lack of interest and also because of impending strategic change respectively. The point to note is that each division of any firm might differ in its standards and the external messages given out by them. The frustration lies in being told the problem but being able to do nothing about it.

Reasons for a 'NO' sale

In many cases, my introductory meeting ended up back at square one, i.e. I did not manage to sell a project. Having heard my summary of services and achievements, the prospects would be somewhat impressed and normally thank me for coming. They would promise to call me when I might be needed. 'Don't call me, I'll call you.' is commonly said, and is generally negative. These negative outcomes can usually be expected. My basic question is – is there really a need for my help or was it just an excuse for a pleasant chat? Probably I have made a convincing case for him to see me in the first place. Sometimes I do use my slightly strong arm to induce a meeting when I can detect some dithering. Some bosses admit that the top could indeed be a very lonely place. Who could you possibly use internally to bounce off your most outrageous ambitions or plans as a sounding board? What would his subordinates think if they were to hear it 'undiluted' from their boss, especially if there is a hint of bad news? The obvious and relatively safe choice is to locate and use a trusted, capable and experienced external confidante. Other possible explanations for negative outcomes are:

The penny has dropped and fear might then emerge regarding the magnitude of their problems. The resulting, unexpected shock upon realisation, however minor, may be too much to handle. For me, this could well turn out to be positive when they realise that something must be done, preferably soon.

There is no personal chemistry between us; i.e. we have not clicked well enough. This might be due to my background (racial, academic and/or professional), cultural outlook or behavioural aspects.

The existence of perceived fear of the consultant, but do believe me – I am not at all frightening to the innocent! I do appreciate that this can appear quite real since few people feel totally relaxed about trusting a stranger with their company's destiny. This is especially the case if they regard it as their baby since they founded it. Also, there is possible fear of losing control, if they are used to having a tight grip on all matters.

On a few occasions, previous bad or negative experiences with other consultants can make it immensely difficult for anyone else, later on, to overturn this strong inbuilt resistance. If things do not work out this time, this consultant's sponsor could be blamed again for making bad decisions, twice this time; potentially a dismissible offence? A kind of 'two strikes and you are out' possibility may also loom true.

My introductory summary (including a sales spiel) was not what they wanted or expected to hear. I might not have accurately located or pushed strongly enough their hot buttons, if there were any at all.

An ulterior motive or objective was there but it was not revealed to me or even hinted sufficiently for me to start probing. It would be a case of trust again, whether it is basically from their gut feel or otherwise.

The prospect misunderstood or misinterpreted my reasons for seeing him. Probably, he might have misheard my verbal phone intro or read something else in my introductory letter. This should never be the case unless the managing director is really green in business.

It happened that it was their bad 'hair day' or maybe a day dominated by 'inauspicious' planetary positions when we met. Who can really guess any unfavourable events that might well have occurred prior to our meeting?

My style or philosophies do not quite fit in within their culture. Perhaps, I have failed to impress sufficiently. Making the best possible impression can be impossible if you are alone and hence without anyone to give you instant feedback after the meeting. Another person present can help to rescue the situation at times. I do admit that my natural approach tends to be direct (to save time), succinct (to avoid misunderstanding) and honest (which is the best policy and easiest in any long term relationship). Basically, what you see is what you get (*wysiwyg*) from me.

Unexpected events may have occurred since I first made contact. These may have changed the level of interest and focus. Other 'unwanted parties' might now be involved, thus affecting the previously positive decision dynamics, and that could make obtaining a deal difficult.

I met the 'wrong' person in the hierarchy and have thus been led around in circles. This is not always controllable since the best contact might be inaccessible at the time or might take a longer time to interest. It could be fate that guided me to make this contact and no one else is accessible. It is really about getting the proverbial foot in the door and making the best of what follows by thinking well on your feet.

The original person I was to meet was fired or left without notifying me. Thus I was directed to see someone else instead. This has happened several times. Invariably, it is not the same and it does not have the same magnitude of positive impact expected. Having made some sort of contact initially, it is better to keep some form of contact fresh in that firm.

Many companies erroneously believe that only in-house experts could be effective.
There are well-known pros and cons here. Typically, the in-house camp naturally say:
- Retain invaluable learning
- Easier to control an employee than an outsider
- More cost effective in the long run (at least on paper to satisfy the money person)
- Keep it internally for confidentiality reasons
- Outsiders do not and cannot possibly understand their issues as well
- Outsiders may not have the necessary industry sector knowledge to be really effective

As an external consultant, I would counter by saying:
- External expertise can bring in fresh (already proven elsewhere) and objective viewpoints
- External expertise can be more time effective, diligent and conscientious due to the commercial pressure to perform

- We can focus on specific issues or achieving identified objectives
- We can act as a temporary resource and hence we are not an ongoing overhead
- Many good ideas that originate from within might well be ignored ('A prophet is never listened to in its own land!') – this happens often and is easy to confirm
- Time is unavailable to train someone internally
- Our extensive network is a goldmine of hidden resources and knowledge

It can be very painful to swallow the 'I have failed pill' and accept fresh, possibly stressful approaches. Losing face is something to be avoided at all costs by more sensitive souls. This issue invariably involves big egos and the realisation that internal failures are common since not everyone can see the timber for the forest every time.

The timing was imperfect as the target organisation might be in a state of flux, with changes beyond control etc. To me, this is a very common excuse to do nothing and potentially, a dangerous situation for the prospect. Changes invariably necessitate the making of tough decisions, often involving emotional factors. Unfortunately for some people, half-baked ideas can be born out of succumbing to the sheer pressure to act prematurely, without conducting good, critical, impartial risk analysis.

They were already employing consultants in a number of similar areas. This is really tough luck, my friend! But, 'are they effective?' could be the best question to ask in this situation. For the user, it may be a case of better the devil you know, rather than taking a chance with someone off the streets. However, after some length of exposure to the same advisers, the approach and ideas can become somewhat stale, possibly accompanied by a marked reduction in overall effectiveness. Perhaps it is then time for a refreshing change or booster.

Your targets are now under new owners, sometimes, bigger corporations with their own significant, internal resources (a probable development since the initial meeting). This is a rather hard one to overcome unless you detect chinks of dissatisfaction amongst the ranks. It seems easier to use the shared internal resources than having to reduce one's own budget. A choice with minimum hassle and costs may seem preferable. Who would dare to stick his head above the parapet and behave differently? However, it is always worth keeping an eye for sizeable crumbs that might fall your way.

The father, owner or children were not interested in gains that might be possible within an 'improvement' programme. This is another difficult one to handle since blood is normally thicker than water. Again, working hard to get recognised and accepted would seem the only solution. Typically, a long haul can be expected before a non-committal 'yes' may be heard. But how deep is your patience well?

The rest of the management team was happy with the way things were and could not see a strong need to change. Changes are always perceived and expected to be stressful; so is there a good solution or substitute action to lessen this pain? This is rather similar to the above. But things can change for the better, resulting in more positive opportunities. But the real question is, is there anyone who would dare rock the boat? What might be the resulting outcomes? Are these attractive to have?

Other 'non-productive' episodes

I felt somewhat optimistic when I met up with a general manager of an airport services business. He was trying to implement change amidst strong internal opposition in a highly unionised environment. Unfortunately, he was a victim of a merger soon after our meeting. He left quite suddenly without any traceable information on his current whereabouts! Possibly, his strategies were sound but he might be too late and was probably incapable of managing the change process single-handedly. I contacted his boss (and his successor) but he was not keen to meet, citing cost as the main reason. I did doubt his response since I had good information about his company obtained earlier on from his ex-GM. It turned out that this company soon went into administration, not long after our last telephone conversations. Sometimes people prefer to put on a brave face amidst all the heavy odds. Unfortunately for them, their tact could well subsequently tar their otherwise impeccable image and reputation.

The filtered water business has always caught my attention because there would be no life without water. Despite the well-publicised fact that tap water in Britain is normally good enough to drink, many would willingly pay for delivered bottled water, or install filtration to mains water for their companies. There are several such water businesses around and the following is one interesting example.

One day at a public show I met a managing director with an MBA. She had managed to fob me off for several months through various reasons – not being around, off travelling, building the northern sales team etc. About two years later, I discovered that she had left and entered the teaching profession. I had a short meeting with her successor, a highly-strung gentleman. Sad to say, being new, he had to prove himself to his Israeli masters, admitting that his tight finances would not allow him to justify the use of external services at the moment. Well, there might be some hope in the future, I thought. For completeness, I must add that I had to bypass one of his highly curt male 'receptionists' to get through to him. In a way, I do sympathise with such highly competitive businesses where offering initial trials of free water is common practice. I did get to see him for 20 minutes or so. According to him, his Israeli masters would not approve of paying for any external investment at this early stage. This was understandable as it would probably show him off in a bad light, it seemed. Obviously, that would be disastrous for him during his probationary period.

My contact with another airport maintenance company (east of London) had an interesting twist. I met its managing director at a public event and he seemed keen to follow up. After cancelling one appointment at the last minute (unplanned board meeting), I did visit him on site to learn about his situation. Apparently his margin was 1% below his industry norm and he was hence motivated to achieve at least that for his site. Ultimately, he was keen on improving his internal process efficiencies and reducing costs. So, we agreed another date for me to discuss my proposal and also to walk around his operational areas. Since it was some way from my base, I phoned him up the day before our proposed second meeting. Can you guess what he said on the phone? He seemed annoyed that I had not sent him my proposal for him to look at beforehand. He wondered whether I was still interested in helping him. This was certainly news to me. Checking through my notes did not reveal such a request. Nevertheless, I did not go as planned but sent him my proposal for his approval. Days later, he informed me that his managers had pleaded with him for the opportunity to give them a chance to improve things themselves. He agreed to this and asked me to contact him in six months' time when he would review the situation. Effectively, I had become his change agent or catalyst, virtually free of charge; stimulating the internal efforts and enthusiasm from my proposal! I did have some doubts about his genuineness for help since his boss (according to him) would never have agreed to such an investment. If he had gone ahead, he would have to finance this project without his boss's knowledge or approval. I also did wonder if my efforts would be paid, eventually. Again, I did have a question or two about this managing director's personality and integrity.

A meeting with the managing director of a water-related business took place after the first appointment was postponed due to issues he needed to tackle. We ended the meeting with the expectation of doing a small exercise looking into its management capabilities in two months' time. By being more 'strategic' now, he had actually lost a good degree of control of his ultimate authority. Because of a management reshuffle, this exercise did not materialise. Subsequent contacts were impossible due to him hardly being there or available. Due to my persistent nature, I have not given up hope yet on this case. The last update confirmed that he has now left the company. This saga may well continue with the new players!

One interesting meeting with a frustrating outcome stands out amongst many other examples. A British based IT company, based just outside London near the M40 motorway was suffering from issues relating to their products. According to its CE (an accountant and ex investment banker), product lead times were relatively long (or overdue), morale varied across the company (lowest amongst the software developers) and its software quality was suspect. He also talked about the structure, weak operations and technical failures of almost seventy percent with his technical products. Common sense would scream out to any person of average intelligence that there were some real issues here that need sorting. This CE expressed his wish to see something concrete as the outcome – a perfectly rational expectation. Can you guess what did happen? Subsequently, he emailed saying that I could not possibly add value to his problem. (Why not?) And he did not want to spend any more time on it, i.e. he declined to see my proposal. In fact he had only spent just over an hour in the initial meeting. There are at least two possible explanations I can think of here. He might have been fearful of the recommended actions he would need to accept to rectify the situation. He might have made a mountain out of the molehill of the perceived problems and may now desperately want to avoid further commitment! He might be suffering from an uncontrollable type of personality schism, potentially giving him extreme inflexibility in his decision making! There was another clue. I persuaded him to see me after having first written to him. He did warn that it would be a waste of both our time and that he could not afford my services. Mind you, his background was in finance!

There have been a few occasions when several members of the prospective company would see me together in the first meeting. In one such case, a marine products manufacturer south of London, the vice president, his operations director and HR manager had a 35-minute meeting with me. As it was an established company with British, US and German origins, I did not expect an easy sell. The VP claimed to have a vision and several good strategies in place. His operations director expressed scepticism about achieving tangible results, based on his past exposure, which was limited to a few consultants. Fortunately, we ended the meeting with the VP suggesting that I should make contact again in January, when they would be planning and budgeting for the next year. This would be regarded as a warm prospect in my list. According to the HR manager, the latest update was not positive and the VP never seemed to be around either! My personal impression of the place was one of gloom and a lack of motivation. The energy was certainly missing.

The sequel to the above was interesting but nothing else. The above VP had suggested I call him again at a better time, but the latter proved difficult to achieve due to his long absences! His operations director again mentioned that his company would be unlikely to use consultants. His colleague, the HR manager informed me that she had not finalised her requirements and was working with a limited budget for external projects. So, what should I make of all that? Probably, this is another time waster.

Here is an interesting and unique example. A fellow London Business School (LBS) MBA graduate had agreed to meet me in central London at 1500 hours. Typically, I aim to achieve more than one purpose whenever I am in London. Full of positive expectation, I turned up at 1445 hours and David told me of this emergency meeting with his Chief Executive (of C...) in an hour's time. He did email me earlier, but at 1339, just 161 minutes before our scheduled meeting! To be fair, he did meet me again (properly this time, but rather secretly, next door in a café) a few days later, asking me to quote for some personnel selection work. This has failed to materialise into anything so far because of his colleagues' preference to use their internal HR skills. This saga ended when this company was taken over by a more aggressive telecoms competitor.

Through a network, I was asked to visit a leading Asian food manufacturer based far from London. My associate accompanied me hoping to increase our chances. This was the result of over six months of phone calls since the last incumbent (operations director) had left. The meeting resulted in a request for a proposal for shop floor training in various hands-on world class techniques to reduce their costs, improve workforce flexibility and efficiency. The proposal was presented and discussed with his production manager. Subsequent phone conversations concluded that there was insufficient time available to pursue since they had had a 'hard' year (i.e. financially meagre) and they asked to be contacted next year. The main problem seems to be their indecision, fire-fighting modes, lack of priority given to this project and the unexpected demands from their customers (low-end supermarkets). I have also deduced that perhaps costs/expense might be an important factor in this particular business culture. Another associate did warn me that the female CEO founder was known to be quite autocratic and difficult. Perhaps a meeting with her might help on this occasion. But she was not often around and making a journey of several hundred miles for a relatively small project seemed somewhat unjustified. As expected, she did not respond to my introductory letter either.

Another case involved a French managing director in a small hi-tech business, who had agreed to meet me in London. I turned up on time and was shown to a glass-sided meeting room by the receptionist. This managing director rushed in within two minutes of my arrival. He mumbled about there being a mistake since he was then meeting his bankers at the same time. I had, however, spoken to him on the phone and confirmed the appointment verbally about two weeks earlier. He might not have entered it in his diary – a fact supported by his receptionist and most certainly not my fault. Sad to say, my subsequent efforts to make another appointment have been unsuccessful so far. *C'est la vie*, indeed! It is another deletion from my records.

Once I turned up at a building consultancy based in the northern Home Counties but was told by the harassed looking managing director that his father had just died. My sincere sympathies to him of course, but business must surely carry on as normally as possible. 'No one is indispensable' has been a commonly repeated statement of mine; although temporary inconvenience might result. How about a simple courtesy call to inform me not to come? That would have saved me an 80-mile trek and two hours' of driving. This seemed to be just another case of a 'non-tough' person in charge – a round peg in an oval hole. A previous meeting with him had shown some promise, hence my follow up effort two years later, tinted with a little optimism.

Many of my target companies have been in the scientific, technical or engineering industries. As a Chartered Engineer, I do believe that my personality traits, natural attitudes and relevant technical type experience resonate naturally well with these cultures. I do have much success in terms of projects with these categories. However, there have also been some rejections. Looking around, there are not many consultants who have a similar technical background. Many tend to remain as technical specialists and not venture into the management or commercial disciplines. Armed with the MBA, some have indeed become more adventurous.

A partner a PhD) in a small scientific company, a competitor of Rentokil, confided that they had no sales team and strategy and had thus suffered from low profitability. He had no time and also admitted that motivation was rather lacking. Needless to say, his other partners were disinterested in doing anything about their plight. Probably it would be a case of 'hello' and 'goodbye forever' to a very lame duck.

I met the managing director of a handling equipment company in 1995 who was in his 60s. According to him, being the only shareholder, life was definitely lonely and difficult. Margins had been poor but he had a good reason to be optimistic. His daughter, who had majored in marketing, would help him. Somehow, he had lost a real sense of direction and strategy. Subsequent phone calls resulted in nothing since he had decided to let his daughter tackle those issues herself. Is it always the best strategy to leave things totally in the hands of the family? In this case, at least would she be invaluable as far as marketing goes? Perhaps it is the case of 'better the devil you know' and 'blood is thicker than water'. Surveys have regularly confirmed that few family businesses prosper beyond the third generation. Leaving his company in relatively green hands may well increase this probability.

In the same year, I visited a firm hiring out photographic equipment and met the group's chairman. They were 100 strong and he commented that 'everybody sells' in his company. In his opinion, he had a reasonably flat company. His approach was to deal directly with his customers and avoid small orders. He even typed his own letters and claimed to have no problems!

Another example concerns a medium-sized company based in an industrial estate fairly near to Hangar Lane, London. Essentially they supply plastics components. My first meeting with the managing director was cordial and seemed rather promising, I thought. He was interested in launching process re-engineering (BPR) throughout his company. This meeting led to several individual meetings with his management team to help formulate my BPR proposal. It all seemed rather positive but the job went to someone the managing director had used previously – 'a real BPR expert', I was informed. Was this an apparent case of someone getting a free ride using my proposal as their guidelines? It will be interesting for me to find out whether any real changes have occurred there and whether the results have met his expectations. It is on my target list of companies to contact since there is always the possibility of a few large crumbs dropping my way.

One multimillion-pound engineering business was a target. I met the managing director on the eve of another merger with another well-known business. We had an interesting conversation about his previous merger activities and the impending one. He had planned to close and merge offices, thus obtaining acceptance to change, relocation etc was his main objective. Maintaining a high motivation level was important to him. His apparent need was for someone to double-check his current plans to ensure total success. Somehow, my proposal was not taken up because they had covered those areas too, according to his internal staff. It was another case of 'keep in touch for the future'. Subsequently, I learnt that my contact had left and the reason could be interesting.

A specialist games table manufacturer, stockist and restorer (based far from London) was another interesting prospect. I met the elderly father (owner) at a public event but ended up driving a total of 110 miles to see his son instead. Apparently the father could not make it back in time to see me. This was a probable indication of how the father worked and his attitudes. The son seemed sensible in what he wanted to do: he was focusing on reducing costs and achieving more sales. However, in my second visit, I met the father, who took me in his 'powerful' banger down some country lanes where he proudly showed off to me his new factory site – an old farm with several buildings. No deal was agreed due to their lack of cash but I did meet two rather interesting characters whom I shall probably not forget. I might have missed an opportunity there, but, what was it? Perhaps there was a kind of hook, an opportunity to invest some time there for nothing on the basis of hope for some sort of reward later. My guts tell me that I would not be 100% at ease if I were to end up working for this company.

One day, I decided to try acquiring a client in the health drink business, in elderflower production, to be precise. With just 20 staff then, it was a family business located in a nice part of South-East England ('the garden of England'). The owner's concern lay in his small-scale factory, mainly about his production manager. He explained his grandiose ambitions to expand via sales to supermarkets etc. This contact failed to materialise into any work despite my many follow-up phone calls. It was a case of the managing director/owner mulling over my ideas, his options, and then reorganising his set up to suit his final decisions. Unfortunately, his 'planning' appeared to have been supported by flawed assumptions. Perhaps I should charge a fee for exploring prospects' needs and in suggesting possible options. At least my time and effort would then be partly rewarded. Since then, I have seen glimpses of this owner in public, but as far as I am concerned, he is now non-existent and is no longer classified even as a tepid prospect. I have also noticed that his somewhat wiser competitors had overtaken him and prospered.

I invested three days hoping to help a well-known buildings trade association, which was located somewhere off the M4 corridor. It started with meeting a fellow alumnus of mine from LBS and his marketing director. There were subsequent meetings with the chief executive and two other directors. However, they (more likely the CE, I guess) rejected my proposal on grounds that they were already taking some appropriate action. This did not come as a total surprise since there were hints given earlier on that they were a cynical lot, preferring to amble along, and that it would take significant persuasion for them to part with their cash. Personally, it was a good learning experience with some interesting insights, which I could make good use of elsewhere. I managed to confirm some of my hypotheses on personalities too (see Chapter 8 for outline info). A good possibility would be to check if their competitors were interested in some of my ideas. It seemed a double challenge here for me – making the contacts and inducing the initial interest.

Non-white prospects

As a fairly rare British consultant of Chinese origin, you would have thought that many of my clients would be of South-East Asian or Oriental origin. Sadly, this has not been the case and I am also personally surprised by this. There might be good reasons, which even I have not quite fathomed properly yet. For pragmatic reasons of not wasting my time, I have decided to avoid contacting such businesses in future.

Perhaps my largely Western education and training have been largely responsible for this conclusion. This does not mean avoiding any serious invitation to meet. My brother-in-law has observed that fellow Malaysians might typically regard me as a 'banana', one bearing whitish internal flesh with a yellowish skin! It does not sound complimentary at all but it does imply that despite being fairly anglicised, deep down we (Chinese) are probably still the same. My attitudes are probably modified by my knowledge and experience. Perhaps a few examples would help to explain.

Many Taiwanese and Hong Kong (Chinese) companies have set up in England to take advantage of the geographical, financial, market and cultural advantages. I have been to at least three small companies just outside North London. Typically, they are fairly frank in explaining the issues and challenges of their firms. However, for various reasons of cost, timing and perhaps pride, few took up my offer of help. In Eastern terms, seeking external advice or help at a senior level could amount to a loss of face, something to be avoided by the more sensitive and the traditionalists. Perhaps, if one of my Caucasian associates were to be sent to make contact with these people, things might have turned out better for me.

Here is an interesting true story. There was a London based Indian company, which had bid successfully for a day of my consulting service from a fund-raising auction at my son's independent school. I had a meeting with their senior director to discuss his requirements. We ended agreeing that he would contact me again in the near future. I have been waiting for at least 12 years, and, so far, I have heard zilch. Mind you, the amount he had donated was probably insignificant.

Hitherto, it has also seemed impossible to convince Japanese managing directors to buy from me too. Many have been fairly courteous when they have first been approached. Despite having good rapport in our meetings, there have always been 'good' reasons for not taking things further. It might be timing, their satisfaction with the current status, organisational change, and lack of perceived urgency were the usual reasons given. I do wonder if it would have helped if I were conversant with the Japanese language or if I were a Japanese person myself. Perhaps, from historical and cultural perspectives, the Japanese and Chinese have never been on 100% good terms. Very possibly, again, not wanting to lose face might be a strong reason too. A good Japanese friend of mine commented that deep trust and familiarity must exist before any business can be contemplated. Perhaps it is a case of formal authority without individual action. Although I am persistent, investing many months/years for relationship building is not a viable business proposition. As you might say, there may be bigger and tastier fish to catch in the wide seas. As mentioned above, it's sad to say that hitherto, I can only claim to have a client belonging to the Asian (Indian) and Chinese cultures. If anyone fits those categories and wish to be my first client, I will be delighted to help and hence correct my current viewpoint!

However, I must say that I do have an ongoing client based in West England that is a Japanese multinational with its international HQ in Japan. However, its European boss (my client) is British. I am pleased to say that he keeps coming back for more!

Hopefully, the time may come in future that their Japanese subsidiaries will come round to using my skills to help them too. Hitherto, this particular client has been satisfied with my contributions so far in developing his UK organisation.

An Indian business involved with enamelling was interested in boosting its sales but the boss himself did not have the critical knack of selling; having 'no patience', he confessed. I suggested helping him to advertise and recruit a sales person. Even though it was for a relatively small fee, his son thought that they could do it themselves just as effectively. I was brought up by my parents to notice the very hard working ethics of the Indian community and also their tight/strong control over spending of their money.

Through a chance meeting at a friend's barbecue do, I met the personnel director of a medium-sized Japanese bank. We soon met again in his London office. Like most institutions, they had used well-known firms for skills development etc. Having heard about his issues and history of his bank, we concluded that it would be a case of him calling me at the appropriate time. Being an Englishman himself, he felt that his autonomy was strongly limited by his Japanese bosses in Tokyo and the strong Japanese culture of doing things. Subsequently, I discovered that it was the prevalent internal politics and his weak leadership that had caused many of their organisational problems. As expected, he subsequently parted company and their problems remained unresolved. Someone did remark that traditional Japanese institutions are not necessarily well run.

I have also visited the Japanese managing director of a famous Japanese tooling company with a well-known household name. Although it started off very formally, he soon shared with me his concerns about his people. However, again the issue of possibly losing face and cost might have delayed a sale on this occasion. A few years later, this managing director was replaced. This raises the question of how feasible it is to build long term, more productive relationships if Japanese firms have this practice of short tenures of management. It looks as though these senior managers cannot wait to return to Japan after their stressful stints of duty abroad in strange lands!

As an ex-Malaysian Chinese, I thought that one Singaporean firm (consumer products) near Sunbury would be an easy conversion. This has proved not to be the case. I did sense something amiss when the Chinese managing director asked me for a sample report, which I could only partly and reluctantly oblige (for obvious reasons). In the end, he decided that he could do better himself. At our initial meeting, his main comment was 'nothing was going well'. His problems covered a wide range of areas – from low profit and inexperienced staff to bad debt and problems with suppliers. Logically, the next step would be to accept good advice to turn the situation round fairly smartly. Sadly, that was not the outcome in this case and I doubt if the firm still exists. I suspect that this is another instance of the boss offloading his concerns over to a sympathetic listener.

Female prospects

An interesting type of prospect belongs to the female category. Although I might be slightly biased (naturally, since I am a male), and by no means sexist, I have found it relatively more 'difficult' selling my services to female clients. Being intuitive/psychic (according to one clairvoyant), at times, I can sense the slight display of discomfort on their part. Conducting an objective survey might yield some interesting pointers. The bottom line is that no direct client, thus far, has been female. Yes, there have been women whom I have subsequently helped within my client organisations but I have only sold my services to male bosses.

Some of the reasons for not using my services specifically given by female prospects:

> 'I will call you but no need to call me'
> 'I will need to talk to ......'
> 'We are in a tight financial situation'
> 'It may be a good idea if we talk again in....(but invariably, stating 'no promise')
> 'I will bear you in mind for the future'
> 'I would like to see you but.....'
> 'My hands are tied as regards doing something about....'
> 'Things are changing and will be some time before we can define.....'

I suspect that you might need a special type of personality to acquire a female client. My partner did remark that women are probably more sensitive generally in every aspect of the interactions. Since the majority of my work involves resolving people type issues, these ladies might feel happier or more comfortable opening themselves up psychologically to fellow female helpers. I am not surprised that perhaps a few of the latter might well be already on their lists or networks. They may also prefer the consensus or 'touchy feely' approach to decision making, thereby taking a longer time to say 'yes'. Perhaps if I were slightly more patient and 'charming' at the same time, things might turn out more positively?

At last, the tide might have turned. I planned to meet a female board director of a well-known hygienic services conglomerate soon. Her initial reaction was for me to write in with my details (quite typical) and this has always been fairly standard procedure. As usual, I followed up with several phone calls, and received her response saying that she had not had the time to think about my letter. Weeks later, she did manage to read my letter and agreed to meet me to discuss things further. I put my success in obtaining this appointment to having done some useful initial, independent research in identifying her true need. As she was not the CEO herself, my hopes were not high that I'd be able to convert her into a client. As expected, she left the organisation a few months later. I can only guess that the organisational changes she had mentioned did not turn out to her favour or liking. This was despite her stating assertively that she was a main board director! So what? Being a marketer, she might well have left for another challenge.

A recent meeting involved meeting a female account manager of a Dutch company selling service type software. Her nervous response on the phone did give me a negative feel although I had spoken to her when she was exhibiting. However, we did meet on the pavement of a café opposite her office for about half an hour. Her main need was to be coached. This coach must be able to help her understand the British culture/attitudes and could also form a bridge with her

Dutch bosses. As expected, I could not fulfil this totally and she said she would put me high on the list when they grew bigger or when she could afford my services.

I visited a well-established engineering company in St Albans on at least three occasions over the years. This was because of several top-level management changes. Probably, I should have taken notice of an A4 display, which in effect said, 'We do not know you......so, why we should we buy from you...'. Did they buy? Also, the company occupied a large building made of timber. You have guessed correctly: they never did buy! The last managing director was powerless to use my skills because they had by then become part of a large mechanical engineering group based in the Midlands which supposedly 'has all the usual resources in-house'. The latter remark is quite a common response from fairly large organisations. Nevertheless, it does not necessarily follow that they are achieving excellence in all areas either. Being a large company means that there might be weak links in their armour. Hence it is never my conscious policy to pursue the larger fish if everything else is equal or smaller ones seem available. These bigger prospects tend to have attitudes or cultural issues that make it harder to sell to. They may genuinely feel that, due to their size, there would be nothing in their business which they cannot handle themselves. If they lack an organisational man, there is nothing to stop them from hiring another.

Other variants – multiple faces, keep-In-touch, micro business etc

Some of the prospects I have met have been helpful. One of these was a building chemical products firm in Buckinghamshire. As usual, I got to hear virtually the whole gamut of the organisational and commercial issues from this managing director. They included cultural differences of his two sales forces, supply chain inefficiencies and poor motivation of his people. Despite having put in some fairly serious efforts, his chief executive was a rather reluctant, would-be customer. In the end, this managing director migrated to the Antipodes. Before he left, he did give me some contact names for business development purposes. Unfortunately, his successor has shown total disinterest in response to my several direct approaches.

An interesting variant in terms of first meetings involves meeting more than one person together in the same room. Most of these have been a waste of my time. My impression is that they would appear to strongly advocate power sharing or consensus in front of me. From a cynic's view, they would want a witness to the discussion and probably felt safer by virtue of not being alone in case they might commit themselves inadvertently. Ultimately, with nobody in real control and since they themselves might have differing objectives, it can be difficult to expect a clear-cut decision even from a couple or triumvirate. From a selling perspective, it is a complex task trying to ascertain their individual priorities and needs. You would also need, in a short time, to thoroughly convince several prospects simultaneously. A possible strategy would be to focus on the most senior decision maker.

One case concerned a labelling company in the western part of England. I met their European head and financial controller. They had collaborated with Reading University and claimed to have used the services of a famous American sales company. We ended up agreeing to keep in touch and that was virtually 10 years' ago! Obviously, keeping in touch is fine but a line has to be drawn if you receive nothing more than a very tepid buying signal. Realistically, how many contacts can one keep in touch with?

To be accurate and fair, you should not be facetious and dismiss the invitation to keep in touch. It is an indication of some interest with future potential of doing business. To put things into some perspective, how much mental effort should you put into a business relationship? A good friend and associate once said, 'It could be time to move on to others'. Correct, there are so many other potentially good clients, who may literally be just waiting for me to make contact with them.

Personally, I have gained more than a handful of new clients by persisting via the 'keep in touch' mode. It might be a matter of good timing or it might be that the other party would need to build sufficient confidence before agreeing to accept help. It is easy to appreciate the risk a client takes by taking into his confidence a total stranger.

There have only been a few occasions when a project materialises after 'keeping contact' for several weeks or after more than five serial phone calls have been made. Making the decision of whether to keep phoning can be crucial here. Knowing your contacts well helps in determining their degree of sincerity or seriousness. Those who perpetually ignore your messages or sound 'cold' should be put at the bottom of your list.

Another example concerns a Japanese electronics firm based near Heathrow Airport. I met their Japanese managing director and financial director together. They were keen to improve the selling competences of their sales force. As mentioned earlier, for most Japanese firms, it is a fruitless venture due to their 'wait and see' and rather wary attitude. Another possible reason might be their reluctance to justify to their staff employing outside expertise – the loss of face dilemma again. Being a relatively new potential supplier does not help either.

Recently, I met a director of a construction firm (based in Essex), who was accompanied by a fresh MBA graduate. The former had expressed interest in reducing costs in their processes. Their strategy was to use consultants on specific areas only (seemed fair enough) and relying mainly on in-house resources for most of their initiatives. Eight months later (i.e. having lost months of potential improvements), they were still trying their skills in process improvements in-house! It was rumoured that they were struggling financially. This director has since left for Australia (sunnier climes?) and my aim now is to contact his chairman.

I met an outwardly 'cold mannered' director of a glass converting company at a public gathering. Subsequently, we arranged to meet but he phoned at the last minute cancelling our appointment, citing absent staff as the reason. However, we met two months later, together with his brother and office manager. There were needs to improve upon their poor customer relationships and organisational structure. We agreed to meet again soon to consider my proposal. However, he phoned me to cancel, saying that they had decided not to go ahead this time. Thankfully, this last minute change of mind does not happen too often. Time spent drafting the proposal would have been totally futile. I would have more pleasure spending the time honing my golf swing in the fresh air or in browsing in antique fairs. Looking back, I did remember this director reacting uncomfortably when internal issues were discussed. This is probably a case of not being willing to change for the better. That was his prerogative.

A success story

Very occasionally, I have struck gold if not silver gilt (i.e. gold plating on base silver) – concluding deals in the first meeting. This can happen if the right chord was struck, probably making the right impressions, saying the right words or things, and if I was empathic and catching my client in the right (buying) mood. In such cases, the need must be clear-cut, very real and urgent. My target will have more than half decided to act. The perceived cost involved would also need to be justified or to be acceptable to them. These are normally cases when I am also civilly offered a drink, albeit only just plain water since I could be allergic to coffee and certain teas.

A success story involved my meeting the managing director of a subsidiary of a US company, which offered object software related solutions. They were located just off the M4 motorway. The managing director's initial answers to most of my questions gave the impression of a hunky-dory situation within his company. However, on further probing he did admit some weaknesses in the commercial areas. Later, I did a project successfully for him offering him useful, objective and insightful ideas. I even helped him to interview and recruit his telesales staff. Due to his laid-back approach and slightly unconventional management style, a few of his problems did grow to become rather complex. As an adviser, you can't be there full time and be told every conceivable problem. Apparently, he was forced out by his US president for one or two obscure, no doubt legitimate reasons. It was rather sad really. But he did compliment me as being 'intuitive with enormous experience'. He has mysteriously disappeared. Knowing his personality from my profiling, I am not surprised at all.

Sometimes, I might meet the fairly reticent type and I do find this fairly hard going, to say the very least. Not only do they not buy, they give signals that strongly suggest that it was a mistake to see me. However, they are normally those without the guts to say 'No' politely when they are first contacted. It does pay for both parties, sometimes relatively 'handsomely', to be assertive. Indeed, coaching to become more assertive has been a popular request amongst many clients. Put simply, it is about one's rights and good old-fashion fair play.

You may well wonder if I ever make contact with micro businesses; those with less than 10 people. Yes, I have done so but nowadays I would rather not bother if I can help it. The only exception is if someone contacts me directly expressing a strong desire for some help. The main reason is fairly obvious – the owner tends to be entrepreneurial and generally wants to do his own thing, i.e. he has a strong need to run his own show and jealously makes all the decisions (i.e. a classic power culture mentality). They will often manage on a very tight shoestring budget and employ their next of kin to minimise costs. In many cases, these companies would be unwilling and psychologically unable to pay, even though my fees are very modest when compared to the average. Nevertheless they do form a high proportion of UK businesses and are normally targeted by the government's free or subsidised services.

The smallest client I have dealt with was a size of 1 person. One company I approached consisted of just the managing director and his wife, involved with the designing and manufacturing of simple ironmongery. It was a start up in leafy Surrey. Unfortunately, it was one where the managing director's friend had been willing to offer his advice *gratis*. Typical of a start up, it was not enjoying any income stream yet, expecting things to happen using a shoestring philosophy. And in my opinion, it will never do so until a different approach is adopted. It was selling a prototype product for the wine trade without a price list and the manufacturing details would need working out to define the true cost. This is an obvious case of an unrealistic DIY venture, doing it single-handedly and risking customer impatience, confidence and possibly causing alienation.

One interesting company had two persons, a man and his partner. This Oxbridge entrepreneur was obviously bright, since he had managed to design a brilliant IT product. His main obstacle was to convince established and larger companies to buy from him. In such instances, to overcome the inevitably strong buying resistance and project sufficient credibility would be his key to success. Hopefully, they will become a client in the medium term. Meanwhile, I have urged an associate to offer him some marketing support, which could lead to immediate sales. The issue there was their need to obtain this small amount of funding from their existing investors.

I also remember a case near my doorstep, where there was a company with four people; a man (friendly enough guy), his wife, a salesman and an assistant. Basically, there were cash flow problems due to poor sales. Their premises consisted of one big room full of mess (or probably labelled as clutter according to *Feng Shui* experts) and a shared toilet. I was offered the chance to invest in their business and partake of equity but somehow I felt intuitively that it was not really my cup of tea. Their products did not have sufficient differentiation to ensure outright success in the short term.

Asking them to take on new products would prove to be a difficult financial challenge.

I have only one example of a friendly managing director who believed that his Sikh God had always looked after him. It was a five-person business in engineering subcontracting, using equipment that reminded me of my noisy but fulfilling days as a production engineer. His main need was to obtain more business (as in most businesses) for his spare machining capacity and the desire to produce his own products. This could mean reducing his reliance on unpredictable workflow. However, he did not become my client as he relocated a few months later to far away Midlands.

The next example is a 15-strong company in the county of Bucks dealing with adhesives. The managing director was interested in increasing sales and improving his tight margins However, he remarked that he had no budget in mind. In his opinion, there was no urgency, i.e. the hunger or fire was absent in his belly. If there was a fire, it was not hot enough to warn him of any danger. After keeping regular contacts for over two years or so, I had decided to drop him from my warm list. A recent Google search could not locate his company. Well, there was some writing on his walls.

I spoke to the managing director of a recycling business at a business event. Subsequently, I met him to discuss his requirements. Operating as a British subsidiary of a foreign parent, he had made good progress so far. With less than 12 employees and spread out in three different geographical locations meant that time was at a premium and, was thus rather lacking. The immediate perceived need was for someone to design a structured process to produce slicker, more attractive and professional tenders. I offered my proposal to help. Needless to say, the managing director had not quite decided whether to go ahead or not, despite having discussions over several months with his superiors. As a ditherer, he can well wait for me till the time comes when I might feel desperate for his mini project.

Question of 'time'?

The 'time' aspect of first meetings can be interesting. I invariably ask my prospect the time he has allowed for our meeting. For most of the time, I would be given at least 30 minutes, although in many cases a generous hour and more. For the minutes given, this really means that I must compress my key 'speech' drastically to leave some time for asking my questions and to conclude. Occasionally, I have been given as much time as I have needed – a really good buying sign. Less than 20% of my prospects give me unlimited time. This would compensate for them appearing late for our meeting. This would also indicate really genuinely serious interest or someone without the time pressure, which I often encounter in most companies. 'Negative' interest companies are those that just offer me 15 minutes or less. This can only mean that my journey to see them was clearly futile. What could possibly be accomplished or even said in that time? Were these people only interested ing saying hello followed by a rapid goodbye? Fortunately, many allow me more time than they initially specify. These are probably cases when I sound interesting to them and have managed to create possibilities for our mutual benefit.

The worst case was a printed circuit board designer and manufacturer, whose managing director told me that he would have to leave in a few minutes! Obviously, he was not the loser since he claimed to be successful and rather busy.

An example of a 20-minute meeting involved a services company in Uxbridge, where my contact was its development director. He behaved abnormally and was reticent and introverted. My questions about decision-making were met with noticeable efforts on his part, best described as evasive. My suspicion was that he might be on the lookout for a greener field for him to graze rather than seeking help for his company at that time. Hence, our meeting was probably his stratagem to make as many contacts as possible, hoping that I could be the bridge for him to cross over to something better.

The unique combination of a 20-minute meeting and a small company is never a good sign. I can recall one such company (10 people) in the tool hire business in North London. Sales were down, the structure was poor, the proverbial fires were raging virtually everywhere, waiting to be put out by someone. They had lost their agents and their staff had displayed poor loyalty. Despite the above symptoms, which was a recipe for definite disaster, the managing director decided against accepting my help. To them, I would be inclined to say: 'you have made your bed and you deserve to lie on it, whatever the outcome'.

A twist to the subject of time concerns how long I am kept waiting before my prospect appears and shakes my hand. This has varied from seconds to 45 minutes. Someone in the office normally almost immediately contacts those late offenders, who are still offsite. The main acceptable reasons are traffic or earlier meetings being longer than planned. My opinion on this is that unless someone (e.g. the PA) has apologised on his behalf with a good reason, there is really no excuse. On a few occasions, I could have walked out in protest and vowed never to return! It is always a balance of when I should give up any hope of a project. My instinct alerts me to my prospect's attitude as regards the respect I might well receive.

The extreme situation is when my prospect is physically absent and has totally forgotten about our appointment. To compound the matter, sometimes nobody at his office is able to contact him to check his whereabouts. There might be perfectly legitimate reasons for this to occur. It might be possible that he had made a wrong entry or forgot to enter it in his diary. A more cynical response would be that he was full of cowardice or was getting cold feet, even in our warmer English summer.

After first meetings

There are various possibilities after the first meetings. As mentioned, one option is for me to wait for them to call my number. Unsurprisingly, I can count on my two hands the number of those who have called. To me, it would be like sitting behind the counter in the high street, praying that some walkers on the pavement would enter my shop. Usually, I would be asked to call back in the future after they had given our discussions some thought. Sometimes, it was about my contact having to check or discuss with other stakeholders. This could mean another meeting or further suggestions to check again sometime in the future. In most cases, this was neither a good nor welcome sign since this would clearly indicate a lack of serious or urgent interest at that time. There could probably be several projects requiring action or investment for this prospect. It would then be the case of whether mine was at the top of this pile.

Several cases of cowardly managing directors come to mind concerning the above. They would typically not answer subsequent phone calls from me. One example was an Arabic managing director in the stone business in North-West London (off the A406). He had admitted having stress-related problems due to his poor organisational structure, weak sales and poor management skills. Another managing director with various offices had problems with his manufacturing issues in the production and sale of abrasive products.

One managing director in the business of repairing special cars met me twice in a few months. On both occasions, although he had appeared outwardly rather friendly, he would be quite testy and evasive in responding to my probing questions. He would say how very well his company was doing; how he had been trying this and various other actions. His 'get out' routine was having to check or discuss with his business partner, whom I had never met. Another... 'Timewaster'?

I shall say more about plagiarising in the next chapter. For now, I will mention the case of a large well-known construction company based in Slough. I met its eager, youngish manager (responsible for 'continuous improvement') one early morning, telling him my achievements in the popular change/improvement areas. He made copious notes, virtually verbatim, and asked quite intelligent questions. He suggested that I call him to check after his next management review. I did so many times, but he would never return my call. Could he have learnt something, probably quite useful from our first meeting? Perhaps his review had forbidden him to make contacts with me. What could possibly have stopped him from at least saying 'no, thank you' and putting us totally out of our 'waiting' misery?

There was the case of an engineering firm that had negotiated exclusive rights to distribute an engineering device/design. However they did not have the ready and essential knowledge to identify their key customers. Moreover, the current sales force was reluctant to change and refocus – possibly due to fear of the unknown. My huge engineering and business network of contacts could have been useful to him in bringing in, fairly early, a good income stream. But, the managing director deemed my suggested fee 'excessive'. The true reason could be due to the fact that the current marketing/product manager might have objected to being sidelined as a result of my potential involvement. But, I was sure that we could work something out to our mutual advantage. At the same time, it can never be my aim to push anyone out of his job.

It was often the case, and to be expected, that no deal was struck till the second, third or even fourth face to face meeting. The vast majority of clients sign up on my third meeting with them. Out of interest and as a challenge, I felt that it would be nice to acquire a client in the laboratory and biochemical type sector. I was lucky one day when I phoned up the managing director of such a company. His sales director phoned me to change my earlier appointment with his managing director and indicated that he himself would be the more relevant person to deal with. I detected a strong hint of annoyance from him but an interesting and informative meeting with him occurred. Since his managing director would need to approve my involvement, it would make sense for me to confirm the key points with his managing director, which I would be doing soon. Unfortunately, his managing director had failed to keep his appointment with me due to other work priorities. Interestingly, my subsequent contact with the managing director confirmed that his particular interest and emphasis was slightly different from those of his sales director! Meanwhile the sales director had gone off focus temporarily because of planned changes in his HQ of sales strategies. But his managing director again slightly disagreed with this view. Let's hope that they eventually become my new client in spite of this.

Company strengths and weaknesses

If you are a consultant or client, you may be interested in what follows. I thought that a selection of the 'strengths' and 'weaknesses' (previously obtained from a brief verbal SWOT, hence verbatim) mentioned by prospects in my first meetings could be really useful knowledge. These can be potent information that can stimulate your thoughts, particularly if you are involved in a similar industry. If you are in that particular industry, do you share similar weaknesses? How can you acquire those strengths for yourself? Do you wish you have some of their strengths and if so, which and by what means? For most companies, there were entries in both strengths and weaknesses. Some would just mention the weaknesses to emphasise their real concerns. There is a special section in Chapter 3, which lists separately the key concerns only. However, it is interesting to note that, despite their claims to some of these strengths, some have disappeared since my interviews! Please note that the product/service offered is in brackets.

Some of the strengths

Very good staff and attitudes, competitive product (price and meeting needs) (IT data)
Friendly, family company, committed management, high quality (construction)

Superior product (descaler)
Capability to develop software, innovators (software)
Family control, very sound technically, niche, very good development (lighting)
Innovative, trademark, product identification (water)
Good name/database, loyal customers (consumer)
Niche, well-established, worldwide agents, traditional customers (marine products)
'Rolls Royce' of ..., quick turnarounds, can repair and make parts (pump)
Good reputation, largest, good facility (goods handler)
Much autonomy amongst people, mutually supportive, not clock watching (lists broker)
Large size (via acquisitions), good customer loyalty, good product quality (exhibition)
Very collegiate team, informal, strong/'lazy' leader (asset investment)
Amongst the top five worldwide, biggest in Europe, good product range (packaging equipment)
Significant business and presence, good reputation in industry, well established (airport related)
Technical ability, flexibility, dedication, long-term customers (designers)
Good market presence and knowledge, brand leader (food)
Very fast growing, excellent Internet business, good showroom (exercise/health)
Never lost customers, has vision, hands on directors (printing)
Design ethic, do a good job, long-term customers (designers)
Big parent company, very focused, autocratic/strong management (electrical networks)
Famous large parent, established with good credibility (marine)
Hardworking, dedicated, reliable, willing to do anything people (health food)
Quick reaction to market, perceived to be bigger than they were (video)
Good management structure, very good product quality (scientific instruments)

Spread of customers and size of customer base, good accountant (plastics)

Good reputation, high quality product/service, technical intellectual base (scientific plant)

New business plan, people left, new management team (paper)

Small and flexible, good people and products (electrical distributor)

Excellent service, high customer loyalty (metal casting)

Dedication, commitment (mailing equipment)

Strong management team, commercial realism, loyal customers, good quality (engineering)

Personalised service, competitive (aviation)

Good service and delivery, good shop floor skills, problem solvers (point of sale)

Knowledgeable about traffic flow, well trained service team, good organisation (vehicle access)

Good reputation, new premises, more cohesive, better marketing tools, good team (machinists)

Number 1 in blow moulding, big machines (mould manufacturer)

Company's growing at a good rate, good reputation/people/product (pharmaceutical)

Fantastic expertise, best names, loyal staff (solicitors)

Good company history, makes products to order, skilful use of wood and veneers (furniture)

Quality of product, people, service (second to none), very experienced father (glass producer)

Wide range of expertise, good at what they do (graphics)

Specialised, flexible, fast turnround (machinist)

Top quality, innovative products, part of a larger group with long-term outlook (toy supplier)

Reputation for good service, reasonable stock, good products (fire products)

Profitable growth, very good product range and image (electronic systems)

Sound name, well-established, good quality product (kitchen equipment)

Good brand name (resin manufacturer)

Family business, nice working environment (label printer)

High quality, medium to high productivity (vacuum products)

Full scanning range, specialised, high technical capability, broad customer base (documents)

Strong name, pioneer, good range of instruments, cohesive, intelligent managers (instruments)

Technically very up to date, stable workforce (toolmaker)

Good brand name in medical sector (plastics)

Family business, approachable, nice working environment (direct marketing printer)

Reputation, good client base, loyal staff, good skills (map related)

Good people with international perspective, UK based, good knowledge of business (seals)

Reputation for quality products, reasonable profit (furniture)

Unique, good design experience, financial backing from parent company (swimming pools)

Brand name, good distribution network, perceived quality (electrical products)

Offers total solution from design concepts to development, manufacture and installation, backed by big parent, good quality (air systems)

Fully skilled, versatile, spend frugally (machine subcontractors)

Helpful to customers, do specials, design skills (equipment)

People, proven product range, debugged, leading reputation, flexibility (autocue)

Creative, interested in processes/materials, professional delivery, good communications skills, good collection of colleagues – right team (sign designer)

Very relationship oriented, flexible, good doers (software distributors)

Under one roof, good service, team works well (air conditioning)

Quality of product/service, price (value for money), leader (glass producer)

Very good brand name, reasonably stable market, good strategies (cable firm)

Reputation, good client base, loyal staff, good skills (cartographer)

Good skills, varied processes and service to key accounts (glass company)

Good reputation, new premises, better marketing tools, good team (sheet metal)

Innovative products, good reputation and quality (electronics manufacturer)

Innovation, loyal workforce, well trained, has goodwill, very good winches (engineering)

Depot in the North (at York), market leader, best design and technical advice, highest profit margin (plastics)

High profile image, reputation for quality, technical innovation, customised/specification market, premium price (plastics product)

Very good business (for over 100 years), good quality clients, financially strong, good industrial relations, international capabilities, quality engineering, good attitudes (transport)

Technical expertise, professionalism, able to respond quickly, product quality, high conversion ratios, self-financing (engineering services)

Many experienced staff, pretty good service, good products, good position (markers)

Has quality, capacity, sound financially, flexible, staff not frightened (subcontractor)

Good team, well established, very good reputation, very responsive, good purchasing/sourcing, getting the price, fairly broad based, can do many jobs (adhesives)

Willing to develop new products, has EDI, CAD/CAM (steel welders)

Flexibility, knowledge, part of big company, has many support services (building consultancy)

Skills, plant/equipment, knowledge (subcontractor)

Experience, expertise, flexibility (equipment supplier)

Product quality (lasts for years), well known in business (vice supplier)

Large asset base (mainly freehold), stable base of major companies (maintenance)

Good financial control, able to put package together (commercial equipment)

Expertise of two founding members, well-known pedigree and reputation, low overheads, problem solver, has small manufacturing/service area, static sales (instrumentation)

Quality product, sensible pricing, sensible and confident people, young, energetic, highly specialised, above average intelligence (filters)

Parent is top, many OEMs as customers (computers)

Quality of product (best in market), financial strength of parent (scaffolding)

Approachable company, no delay or add in costs, good labour force, high work standards, healthy order book, improving cash flow (building services)

Leading edge products, open company/culture (no bosses) (microwave)

Uniqueness of products, quality of staff (prosthetics)

Sales/marketing skills, quality producer (automation)

Flexibility, service, good quality compared to competition, fairly unique (packaging plant)

Big market (largely not contacted), competitive service, reinvested in plant/machinery, in-house tooling, right pricing, funded from turnover (plastics)

Quick response to problems, quote within 10 days (engineering)

Team of people, core technical strength (metal finishers)

Extremely technical base, young team, diverse products, can be focused (instrumentation)

Established a long time, acceptable quality, secure jobs (fabrics)

Specialised products (niche), good team and image (dental product)

Automated manufacturing, consistent quality, quick new product into market, good marketing and operations, good/sound engineering (valves)

Old, established, experienced workforce, in-house trained, very good name, non-unionised (tools)

Engineering, specialist manufacture of stainless steel (photographic)

Strong production engineering, no unions, good management relationships, good quality, high image, good quality base (chairs)

Loyal staff, autonomous, slick financial control (cut to bone), dynamic people, good business (logistics)

Good, total service, very wide range (light distributor)

Loyal workforce, company has vitality, very good management team, increasing profit, crucial quality, very efficient operations (mats supplier)

Name/goodwill with hospitals, cooperative staff, good morale, 3000 end products, good manufacturing, good customer services (medical supplies)

Good computer systems, good/very broad range of products, very low staff turnover, long term customer contacts, family owned (weighing machines)

Investments in equipment, manufacturing technology, strong asset base, new products, steady expansion/sales growth (instruments)

Broad spectrum covered, marketing strength (water side) (chemicals)

Product profile geared for market, very professional with principals, very good image, excellent customer loyalty (electronics)

Unique product, UK exclusivity, technical skills, covered many industrial sectors (engineers, agents)

First innovator, biggest product range for routing process, product quality, loyalty, good people, market leader (engineering product)

Reputation, financially secure, good workforce and good quality (pottery)

Promotional skills, in niche market as the market leader in two areas.

Knowledge of employees/expertise, market knowledge, product performance (image equipment)

Some very good people, very good company philosophy, very good staff, quality, offering worldwide service, integrity exists, company can be trusted (prosthetics)

Has number of technical specialists, confident to be on time, can do most in-house, good customer loyalty (maintenance)

Very good reputation ('Rolls Royce'), good quality, good relationships with customers (coachbuilder)

Technical engineering, people involved and dedication expected (plastics processor)

Amongst top four in casting as pioneer and leader, known quality, commercially strong (casting)

Broad foot print in industry, few competitors, good cash flow, owns most property (parachutes)

Good team of long-serving people, 24 hour service, well established, good reputation (phone answering service)

Innovative design, fast response, hands on attitudes, short lines of communication (printing)

Sound, detailed experience of people, especially at senior level (aerospace subcontractor)

Brilliant people, products, fast growing (toy manufacturer)

Go ahead, visionary managing director, had courage to push things, take risk, very strong mix of expertise, experience, knowledge (government defence agency)

No equal competitor, well designed and professional products (good range), united team in one direction (lift company)

Good technical team, very flexible, good reputation, pretty responsive (when compared to Microsoft) (IT)

Good focus on customers' wants, very service oriented, good management team (laundry)

Fully skilled workforce, versatile (engineering)

Have 2 complementary businesses (valves manufacturer)

Bends to help customers, offer specials, design skills (engineering)

Personnel, proven product range, bugs knocked out, leading reputation, flexibility on product (studio equipment)

Flexibility, attention to customer satisfaction (telecoms equipment)

Reputation within industry, financially sound company (laboratory testing)

Quality, able to react quickly, skills (machinists)

Experience, knowledge of industry (pharmaceutical (controls)

Well regarded, sales people have latent motivation, well known by other instrument companies (instruments)

Sells solutions to problems, application oriented, effective marketing, very efficient (scientific solutions)

Very good image, excellent support team, very good technical strength, technical leader, very good people (IT)

Market leader, good range of products, strong engineering and marketing, good day-to-day information, good control of bigger clients (computer keyboard)

Quality, good price, friendly and helpful (IT repairs)

Specialised scanning, focussed product and service, uniqueness, very high tech capability, broad customer base, well known, good solid financial base, very strong and good team (imaging)

Very strong name and market share, pioneer, reasonable range of good products, cohesive and intelligent management team (engineering)

Technically up to date, fairly stable workforce (tooling)

Opportunistic, flexible, gives what customers want (lighting)

Good reputation for integrity, helpful, high level of service, lot of time and efforts for after sales service (packaging)

Extremely good reputation, well known for over 34 years, proud of customer care, covers whole of audio visual equipment, three locations, complete package (audio visual).

Brand name, manufactures high specifications and small components, can solve gauging problems (gauges)

Personnel – lots of specialists, company loyalty, operated stocking policy, distributes specialist lamps and designs (lighting)

Knows own capabilities, smart, intelligent, knows actions, belief (architects)

Quality, commitment, speed of response, ability to get work (subcontract engineering)

Good production manager, ability to manage growth, fairly clear plans, enough space (instruments)

Market leader and good name, gets it right – never gives up, dedicated workforce, best machines, good technical base, good praise from customers, good quality system, systematic approach to manufacturing (forming)

Enthusiasm of management team, production performance (paper mill)

Hi-tech customer base, strongish hi-tech strength, good worldwide market penetration (fans)

Product range, company name, experience, strong financial performance, personnel and shop floor skills, good inventions (instruments)

Technical ability with processes, will to invest in things for long term, persevere to get right, good team of people (plastics)

Entered market early, maximum internal understanding, positive cash flow, no external shareholders (IT)

Fast reactions and looks after customers, technically strong, vast base of experience (casting)

Able to take technical requirements for products, work efficiently in timely manner (high tech, IT)

Very strong reputation, high quality output, very good results, ambitious, technical expertise, entrepreneurial drive (SEOS)

Efficient process, value, smart operations (retail IT)

Friendly business, well established, problem solver, widest range of products (displays)

Good brand, international parent, good UK coverage (climate control)

Very good products, good sales staff and not going backwards (filters)

Proactive, solution provider, creative, staff learnt mistakes, innovative (graphics)

All research and development done here, very strong team, good product, clearly identified sales and marketing strategies, very good customer feedback (instruments)

Very loyal workforce, knowledgeable, long service, very good technical base, rock solid image (airways)

Some of the weaknesses

No brand reorganisation, 'oversold' sometimes (IT data)

Invisible board, not keen to tell people what to do, Chairman involved in all areas (construction)

Inability to get message across to customers, no benchmarking/standard (descaler)

Sales/marketing – too many things to get right into market quickly (software)

Old product range, paternalistic, old habits (lighting)

Poor customer service, not lowest cost, internal communications (water)

Not manufacture, has production/scheduling problems, untrained, inexperienced (consumer)

English mentality, high price levels, undifferentiated products, people intensive (marine products)

Very old staff, weak sales, bought in parts at a price (pump)

Complacency, ownership problems, four general managers in four years (goods handler)

Too big to speak to everyone, inflated egos, squeezed margins (lists broker)

Lacks 'sales' culture: low conversion ratio, seasonal business, variable service quality (exhibition)

High overheads, uneasy relationships with partners re: communication (asset investment)

Unsophisticated marketing strategies/tactics, inefficient technical training (packaging equipment)

Not very commercialised, limited market knowledge (airport related)

Poor in developing new business/attracting new customers, low conversion ratio (designers)

Weak market penetration, weak business structure and strategy, disparate processes (food)

Weak structure, customers' views incomplete (exercise/health)

Lacks professionalism, fickle/demanding customers, inter-functional conflicts (printing)

Poor in selling, traditional, lacks time to integrate socially (designers)

Low morale in sales/marketing, bad communications, disjointed structure (electrical network)

Can't plan, poor strategic vision, cyclical business, expensive, dearth of skills, high costs (marine)

Max 2/3 weeks horizon, constantly reactive, no long-term strategy, no management (health food)

Weak communication to potential clients, lack of designers – limited resource) (video)

Poor engineering/sales interface, low productivity, weak marketing (scientific instruments)

People limitations, needs strategic plan, lacks cash, low entry costs (plastics)

Weak in some territories, long product lead times (scientific plant)

Inexperience, conflicts at all levels, poor time management (paper)

Staff turnover, weak career prospects, local competition for people (electrical distributor)

Multinational competitors, fluctuating sales, pricey, low productivity (engineering)

Predictable behaviour, conflict avoidance, weak teamwork (mailing equipment)

Director lacking confidence, some technical problems, conservative, set in ways (metal casting)

No marketing strategy, lack of staff, no structure, lacks direction (aviation)

Poor innovators, low morale, traditional attitudes ('this is how we have always done things') (point of sale)

No 'can do' attitude, weak support, tools lacking, gap in sales (vehicle access)

Weak management, small number of customers, small core skills (machinists)

Unprofitable, one main Luxemburg competitor, lack of staff loyalty (fire products)

Sales people not as a team, one-man company (moulding manufacturer)

Structural concerns, personality conflicts, varied priorities, reliance on suppliers (pharmaceutical)

Attitudes of senior partners, scatter gun marketing, structural issues (solicitor)

Lacks time/planning, need to invest technically (furniture manufacturer)

Lacks storage space, too many things, no priority, weak chain of command (glass producer)

Weak managing director, runs company from day to day, low margins, weak management (graphics)

All subcontract work, not own product (machinist)

Not profitable enough, inefficient processes (toy supplier)

Slow speed of technical take-up, small size compared to the big boys (electronic systems)

Insufficient sales staff and sales, supplier relationships, family conflicts (kitchen equipment)

High fixed costs, reliance on customers, poor visibility to end users (resin manufacturer)

Weak understanding of processes, no time to train, high wastes, supplier costs, missing skills/experience, feared general manager, conservative attitudes, high price (vacuum products)

Weak vision, narrow focus, no marketing expertise, lacks specific experience (documents)

Reluctance to take calculated risk, not diversify and expand range (instruments)

Weak sales, inefficient methods, three sites, one man company (toolmaker)

Expensive products, arrogant image and reliant on direct customers (i.e. not end users) (plastics)

Indispensable key pillar (managing director), i.e. no number two, not moving fast enough (direct marketing printer)

Reliant on few customers, skill base aimed at declining markets, management 'lost', low morale, variable attitudes (map related)

Poor focus after getting orders, too many rules to follow (seals)

Lacks direction, lacks management capability, poor working conditions, complacency (furniture)

Central control of overheads (swimming pools)

Inability to respond quickly, perceived to be expensive (electrical products)

Delivery, lacks orders and good engineering management (air systems)

Lost enthusiasm amongst higher management (machine subcontractors)

Wholly dependent on the managing director, low profits (equipment maker)

Overstock, affected by Gulf War, lacks sales experience, other distractions (autocue)

Marketing, costs reduction, no planning (health products)

Better awareness of competition, time for proposals (lab equipment distributor)

Incompetent leaders, under perform on sales (customer information management)

Under funded, regarded by customers as very expensive, limited space (sign designer)

Weak access to products, limited by suppliers (software distributor)

Not proactive, no new ideas, not learn well, disparate systems (air conditioners)

Poor delivery (glass producer)

Unknown in the field (cable firm)

Expensive due to high cost base, sales effectiveness, 55% effective managing director (son) (windows maker)

Weak planning, excessive paperwork (blinds company)

'Arrogant', slow, expensive, no strategies, office problems (glass company)

Reliance on small number of customers, small core of skills, motivation, conflicts (sheet metal)

Small volume manufacture, emphasis on sales, not marketing (ineffective), recession prone, no loyalty, average product/service quality (electronics manufacturer)

Reliance on family resources, limited finance, handling of one generation to another, CAD rejected, competitive in UK, be more profitable (engineering)

One product per market, cautious private company, expensive guy in computer area (plastics)

Old-fashioned production, complacency, ignorance of emerging technologies, old fashioned attitudes, not achieved budget, slow information flow (plastics product)

Attitudes to customer, no marketing/development, lacks spending on infrastructure, no management succession, lacks team spirit, high absenteeism amongst drivers (transport)

Poor communications, personality weaknesses, confused priorities, no corporate policy, lacks technical staff, no marketing strategy (engineering services)

Staff to assume more responsibility, ineffective marketing, high overheads (markers)

No marketing ability, weak works manager, slow delivery, inaccurate quotes, low morale, limited staff (subcontractor)

Lacks sales force, lack market information, no business strategy/plan, easy management style, needs to be independent (adhesives)

Under utilise intellectual capabilities, stifled by cash flow, price undercutting in domestic markets (steel welders)

Young company, weak in numbers, lack work (building consultancy)

Lack money/work/time, wearing many hats, doing paperwork at weekends, pricey, high-risk jobs, above average reject rate (subcontractor)

Weak, unreliable staff, insufficient people, lack money (overdraft situation), little money made   from engineering (equipment supplier)

Expensive, no marketing strategy (engineering vice supplier)

Naïve management team (lacking skills), not technically adept, weak strategy, faulty computer, quality problems (maintenance)

Wrong marketing, tied to factoring company, high stock levels, lax servicing (commercial supplier)

Broad range, lacks manpower/systems, lacks company plan, limited marketing, barrier between   Directors and workshop, staleness in office (instrumentation)

Undermanned, lacks a salesman, hazy job designs, static revenue (filters)

Battle against conventional product, no corporate strategy, long lead times to convert (scaffolding)

Loose cash control, late negotiating, two not pulling their weight, conflict problems, poor morale, lethargic attitudes, lost customer loyalty (building services)

People limitations – not used to thinking thoroughly to find solutions, had infighting (microwave)

Volatile market, short of capital, poor profits, lost customers due to pricing in NHS, internal ingrained barriers, weak stock control (at many centres) (prosthetics)

Very weak IT, quality of direction, three days to do transactions, high labour, errors (automation)

Sales direction, high costs, negative attitudes, ineffective workforce (packaging plant)

Large loan, limited physical size, can layout more efficiently (plastics)

Lacking in finance, aging workforce, one off specials, ineffective marketing (engineering)

70% of turnover with one customer (metal finishers)

Grown by acquisition, no identity with individual pieces, weak marketing, no forms of intertrading, poor image in technical services (instrumentation)

Lets people down (oversold), poor production flow, not enough capacity, no strategy, no salesman, no loyalty in trade (fabrics)

Lacks capitalisation, much handwork, transition re: methods, not very profitable, overstock, all manual systems, poor manager (dental product)

Slow decisions, lacks new product development, partly static growth (mature market), not strategic sales, average morale (valves)

New tool not patented, being computerised (tools)

No marketing strategy, unpredictable sales, over borrowed, high overheads (photographic)

Limited physical space, no corporate strategy, sales plateau (chairs)

High costs, recruitment problems (overpaid drivers), dogmatic staff, skills shortage, a substantial client (logistics)

Not specialists, labour shortage, poor quality of people, distances between offices, no design department, poor image, low profits, low commitment (distributor)

Lacks older head, need to address communication, vulnerable position as leader, price sensitive (mats supplier)

Strong competition, no strategy, communication difficult, not enough profit, difficult central buying, complicated stock control (medical supplies)

Poor staff attitudes, communication between departments, lacks space, low profits, sales skills, weak electronic knowledge (weighing machines)

Slow output, slow shipping, nervous staff, too many products, slow service, competition from Far East and UK, hard to set up distribution (instruments)

Untrained and high turnover of sales force, cannot distribute to all customers, need to increase sales, slow to deliver, quality can be better (chemicals)

Lacks professional sales and supervisory training (electronics)

Areas are new to current sales force, reluctance to change, traditionally very competitive (engineer, agents)

Low margins, weak finances (engineering product)

Inefficient in fulfilling orders efficiently, lacking formal training and wider experience (pottery)

Low motivation of sales force, poor teamwork and weak cohesion with other functions (laboratory)

UK based only, software processes, weak processes in operations (IT)

Product quality in production engineering/design, high internal rejects/wastage, lacks control over selling/distribution overseas – negative feedback on international service, guidelines missing.

Weak organisational and confused direction, limiting skills development/growth of staff, susceptible to quality of supplies, small team and average delivery performance (imaging equipment)

Internal procedures, selling company to customers, needs to increase understanding (prosthetics)

Not producing enough profit (5%), hence little training on commercial skills, weak in converting quotes to orders (maintenance)

No awareness on how to use company's strengths, when, how and where to market his products, problems with profits, price conscious, competition from ISL (Japanese company) (scientific instruments)

Static sales, high gearing, bad factory, bad delivery, lacking skilled workers, poorly structured, weak cash flow, no stores systems and stock control, no costing, no strategy and objective, less than 5% profit before tax, weak overseas agents, very low morale, high staff turnover, lax timekeeping, blame culture (coachbuilder)

High shop floor labour turnover (12-hour shifts), restricted site, (plastics processor)

Consolidation of industry, loss of customer confidence, cash flow, defence market had gone, commercially aggressive, philosophical change needed (old dogs, new tricks), scarcity of toolmakers, low productivity, high costs, (casting)

Specialist, low-tech manufacture but complicated, lumpy sales, small 'cake size', 20% of profits in rejects (parachutes)

Needs more customers and be more selective, lack quality people, to improve training, difficult to advertise, most expensive, no market research (answering service)

Shortages of skilled and unskilled people, no succession planning, not enough training, high labour and land costs, no stock control, not computerised invoicing (printing)

Next line of management needs training, weak supervisors (aerospace subcontractor)

People (may not adapt), growing pains, products, reliance on research and development, imperfect procedures, flat structure, high overheads, expensive materials, geography affects communications, difficult in sales and marketing for brand awareness (toy manufacturer)

'Not invented here' (NIH) syndrome, poor focus and targeting, unclear end users, poor communications, high staff turnover, risk averse, low productivity, complacency due to civil service culture, research versus customer conflict, non-profit focus, (government defence agency)

Lack of capital to exploit, limited manufacturing resource (lift)

Lacking marketing insights, delivery problems, saturated market, some management skills lacking, hard to acquire new customers, some unhappy customers (IT repairs)

Underinvested, understaffed, no product champion, no strategy, flat structure, conflicts between sales and technical, indecision (IT)

Lacks cash, inefficient operations, price competitive, unreliable equipment, conflicts amongst technical staff, black-and-white attitude of chairman (commercial laundry)

Higher management had enough, lost enthusiasm (engineering)

Restricted working capital, GM failed in some jobs, partner weak in learning and not trusted, bad internal communications with friction, poor quality supplies (valves manufacturer)

Totally dependent on managing director, low profit (engineering)

Overstock, affected by Gulf War, lacking sales experience, diverted by too many interesting things (studio equipment)

Insufficient independence from parent for more rapid response, inadequate management experience, insufficient space (telecoms equipment)

Differentiation with competition – no longer unique (laboratory testing)

Old building – not prestigious, needs more technicians, underfinanced, middle of the road turning and milling (machinists)

Insufficient time to follow up sales leads, weak selling skills, open too many doors, long time trials, tiny company, not keen to expand, unpredictability, need to diversify (controls)

Got internal perception of image (seen as 'weak' by customers), difficult for him as managing director to accept advice, unassertive, loss of direction, flat and stale sales approach, using 50% capacity (instruments)

Inflexibility due to business plan, growing pains, inefficient people management, very low margins, lack of training, reducing sales level (scientific solutions)

Not enough marketing (3% on turnover), not creative product marketing (IT)

Lacks financial director, inability to collect overseas cash, cannot compete with large quantities, just keyboards, very high PR and marketing costs, succession dilemma, conflict between sales and accounts, expensive products, flat sales for two years (computer keyboard)

Not strong vision, been traditional and fairly fixed, lacking expertise, no marketing to relieve sales people, lacks sales experience, (imaging)

Reluctant to take calculated risks – to diversify and broaden product range (engineering)

Sales, methods, on three sites, one-man company (tooling)

Weak financial planning, declining UK market, slow product development, management structure, lacks quality in designs (lighting)

Weak management, sales, administration procedures, lacks sales training (packaging)

Financial, slow to react with business problems, recession, redundancies, sales, profits (audio visual)

Distractions from single direction rather than concentrating on speciality, not knowing enough of competitors (gauges)

Not capitalising on projects/products, not hard enough, sales training, correct literature, not enough advertising, works too long hours (lighting)

Slow response time, wrong staff, needs better site and area, needs constant work, strong competition (architects)

Sales, not seen some customers for five years, being undercut on prices, vulnerability (subcontract engineering)

No personnel manager, no sales and marketing person (instruments)

Highly priced middle management, imperfect mentality of workforce (forming)

Level of people training, poor infrastructure, poorly equipped, very low morale, order book not full, poor reliability (paper mill)

Lack of technical management, low sales (fans)

High working capital, no marketing director, no new products, unclear services, not see far ahead (instruments)

Not easy to extract information from info system, limited experience of cell manufacturing, no customer loyalty, expensive, high rejects and stock, decreasing customer base (plastics)

No preparation for continual growth, no hierarchy, no HR manager, internal politics, weak communications, insufficient sell back at base, how derive solutions, poor meetings (IT)

Unclear direction of future due to environment, element of fear from industry (casting)

Resource issue, average sales, not fully integrated IT system, contract overruns, negative attitudes, weak communications, inefficient operations (high tech, IT)

Lacking process, confusion over roles/responsibilities, lacking time, cost overruns on budget, no analyses, functional spin (SEOS)

One core client – high risk, lacks ability to control, low conversion ratio (retail IT)

Relatively small, self-funding, bad debt losses (displays)

No top team, high staff turnover, autocratic UK style, lacks market focus, no marketing director, poor company image, many competitors, slow growth, no brand image, lack overseas critical mass, weak reward system, weak culture (climate control)

Not following leads/visits, static and mature market, erosion in product range (filters)

Small marketing team, too gentlemanly, some customer complaints, loose specifications, in too late to sell/quote, sales pipeline not well managed (instruments)

Old-fashioned company, not known in depth by others, flat turnover, 'short arms, deep pockets', lacking investment, lean structure (airways)

Ideally, the above should be read in conjunction with the 'concerns' expressed, thus completing the picture. The concerns are summarised in Chapter 3. Armed with the above information on what many firms have regarded as their 'needs', you should have a clearer picture, hence greater accuracy on what to target successfully.

Some time-wasting meetings

From years in dealing with companies, one category of meetings would never seem to result in work. This concerned companies that were performing well enough for them not to experience enough 'pain' in their companies. This meant that their companies varied from doing OK to doing very well. Or, whatever issues they might have, these were regarded as fairly routine problems that did not justify outside intervention. Unfortunately for advisers, many companies would not contemplate external help unless they felt that they themselves had exhausted all possible internal solutions. These prospects were probably in a good mood when I contacted them for a meeting. They may have been thinking along the lines of, 'this sounds like a nice chap; presumably there is no harm seeing him...he may possibly know one or two head-hunters' (for his personal benefit). You must realise by now that getting a face-to-face appointment is normally the first essential step. It is by no means an easy feat. However, there are now niche players who phone me and offer such a service – to find me appointments for a fixed fee. As mentioned earlier, this method has its disadvantages.

Another possible explanation to some agreeing to meet could be that these were people who would enjoy sharing the good news and successes of their companies. Such meetings might be regarded as a mini PR exercise for them to spread the words. Thus, it could be an opportunity for free promotion and publicity about themselves, for their products via me. Who knows what would follow next; I might even introduce valuable business to them. Unfortunately for them, this is unlikely to happen as my aim is to help them by utilising my services. However, whenever appropriate, I am normally quite happy to do someone a favour.

It is worth mentioning that I had come across a few 'self interest' type cases, as hinted above. These were situations where the managing director or senior manager probably had some inkling that they might be leaving their current positions. Leaving to work as what, you might well ask. Possibly to become independent consultants, like myself, adding to the already infinite list of competitors. They would typically ask me several questions concerning the whys, wherefores, fee rates etc. As expected, a few moons later, I would not at all be surprised to hear that so and so had now left and was now working as an independent consultant, sometimes helping their previous employers. Personally, such a person should strictly be termed as a pseudo-consultant. In some cases, this type could very likely tarnish the good names of the more established professionals. A switch of profession often necessitates climbing onto a new learning curve. Consulting is no different.

Over the years, I have only met one clear-cut situation where the director was only interested and insisted in payment by results. Others had queried but withdrew their wish when they heard my views on this approach and my reasonable conditions. This example related to a furniture manufacturer, based east of London. Basically, his on-time delivery figure was already around 94.5% – an admirable achievement by any standards. To be rewarded from the savings, I would need to achieve an average of 98% over a six-week period. I declined because there could potentially be several external factors outside my control. More importantly, I would not be given 100% authority, i.e. full executive control over all the internal processes and decision-making. They, like everyone else, wanted fresh ideas, but they would not get them at my expense, no way, Matey! Everyone who knows me will tell you that I enjoy tackling real challenges but only realistic ones, and where I will be modestly rewarded.

More success stories

Obviously not all first meetings prove fruitless. If that were the case, I would not have acquired any clients! As mentioned, it is a numbers game where making a predicted outcome is virtually impossible. So, it is time to relate a few examples of first meetings that resulted in work. I shall reveal more substance in terms of project content later on.

One of my early clients came from the teleconferencing sector. My first contact was with the chairman who passed me onto his managing director. This was one of a few occasions that worked out well. The managing director was impressed by my credentials and took an immediate liking to my approach. He was the recipient of several coaching sessions, which boosted his competencies substantially. Subsequently, he moved on to a bigger role elsewhere in the same industry.

Another client required three meetings over a number of years before he finally bit the bullet. For him, it was really a case of using my persistence and a gradual build up of trust. After all, his IT company was effectively his baby and letting a stranger in to 'nanny' his 'family' did take plenty of coaxing. It did not help that he had to suffer some attitudinal issues amongst his senior people.

The owner and managing director, with a French-sounding name accepted my suggestion for a meeting. This resulted in nothing due to various changes taking place then. However, about a year later, I struck 'silver' in our second meeting. He was probably impressed by my persistence and our fairly compatible personal chemistry. I am pleased to note that I am still remembered today by the current managing director.

I acquired one client by virtue of both of us having attended a similar alumni function at London Business School, though we did not actually meet at the event. Meetings at his office convinced him of my potential skills in helping him effect some attitudinal and operational changes in his company. Again, this was probably a case of 'birds of a feather flock together'.

It took me several years of professional courting of a logistics firm before I was cautiously welcomed in to help. Earlier on, I had made contact with the key directors in various functions connected with my wife's involvement. Again, I think that it was a case of getting to become a more familiar face in my client's eyes that tipped the balance in my favour. Someone in this industry commented that, due to natural occurring cliques and fairly closed circles (a common feature), it was difficult for an outsider to break in. Again, patience and good tenacity paid off very handsomely.

Still an active client of mine, I met this particular 'multinational' client seven years ago in London before he expanded and relocated to their HQ in Gloucester. Our first meeting was warm, friendly and he accepted my proposal on the spot to help him evaluate his sales force's effectiveness. I would put it down to personal chemistry and that my client obviously clearly knew what he wanted and took a chance with me! It seems that he has no regrets since I have helped him on several occasions with his management and organisational design issues.

One client virtually engaged me immediately after meeting him in a trade show in the IT sector. I did need to convince his fellow directors of my contribution of potential value though. He would remember my words consisting of 'the alarm bells were ringing loud and clear' for him then. I succeeded in strengthening his organisational structure, strategies and corporate worth before it was sold off a few years later. This managing director is now with another bigger IT firm. Naturally, I have made contact with his boss there. As the latter was an ex-consultant, I am not overly optimistic. This is because most consultants (especially the pseudo ones) tend to view fellow consultants in a fairly negative light.

I met the father of one client a few years earlier. Interestingly enough, the son then, according to my contact, the father, did not want my involvement. However, later on, when their circumstances had seriously worsened, the son agreed to meet me to discuss business. At that time, the son had 'fired' the father and had also drastically downsized his work force. It was a case of over indulgence on the part of the senior in making costly technological investments, probably at the expense of losing good customer focus. I did help but I guess that it was probably too late to make a significant impact.

An engineering company involved with castings was amongst my warmest prospects. Our first meeting went very well when I was amazed by the many frank statements and 'confessions' of modesty made by the managing director. In this case, being a Chartered Engineer and having good knowledge of the shop floor set up were advantageous in helping me secure the work.

The NO-NOs

I will end this chapter with examples of industries in which I have not succeeded (thus far) in acquiring clients.

The first one is related to printing. I once worked as a general manager, running a printed plastics business but that did not seem to help! One example was a company with a dozen people. They relied on referrals for their orders, which were not priced cheaply. However, their intimate knowledge of their 20-odd customers was low; a classic case pointing to the need of conducting a customer survey exercise. The latter was suggested but was turned down. They had preferred to muddle along instead. Other printing companies I had approached seemed to have a fatalistic tendency whereby the likelihood of embracing a successful change was deemed low. Another mindset seemed to revolve round the need to keep the main focus on cost cutting and nothing else. It is understandable as a strategy for survival but investing in differentiation can well be a more profitable one for the medium term. Ultimately, basing one's strategy on minimum costs alone can mean dangerous exclusions of other key factors.

I was asked to follow a lead based in East England from a network contact. It concerned meeting a general manager of a large poultry processor with an associate. It turned out to be a lengthy involvement of interviews, tour of his plant and a subsequent return visit to see his key managers. Having benefited from consultants a few years ago, I thought that they would now be fairly receptive for 'more'. We offered a highly focused proposal based on our first meeting. In effect, he wanted to be given ideas for him to consider or adopt as his next phase of strategic development. Unfortunately, it turned out to be a waste of our efforts. He expected ideas of best practices and their locations etc. beforehand so that he could evaluate them for himself before proceeding with our proposal, i.e. free information. It was our intention to be paid by him to investigate current best practices for him to consider! Our suggestion to meet his board directors was turned down for very obscure reasons. Having interviewed his dozen or so managers it was clear that there were definite needs in various areas. My associate has now taken charge to pursue this lead, but the prospect has since postponed the meetings several times for reasons of bird flu, timing etc. The make and age of this general manager's car did give us a strong clue!

Another difficult industry was banking. One contact was an area corporate manager who had experience of my 'managing change' seminar held especially for a local high school. It happened that my wife was one of its school governors. This manager's interest was about improving sales and commercial aspects for his branches. In the end, they (his corporate bosses) decided to do it in-house. This was half expected since most established banks have their own training and learning resources. How effective would they be, as compared to a more impartial and externally-based expert would be debatable.

The other example was my dealings with a purchasing executive (external services) of another clearing bank in the City. It seemed to me that things would go round in circles, in terms of who might be interested and who else would decide. It was similar to playing musical chairs within this organisation; probably a way to keep some of the brains busily occupied and thus help sustain a good company size.

I also met a corporate manager of a clearing bank in a networking event. We subsequently met in his West London office. As usual, we exchanged information and he would 'bear me in mind' whenever he might come across his clients that would need my skills. Unfortunately for us, I was disallowed from even repaying him in kind for any referrals, which could possibly come from him in future. There might be an opportunity of some work I think, if I were to approach his immediate superior, a director.

An industry with good potential seems to be the law firms. They seem to be stuck in a type of cultural time warp, probably a situation of their own making. With complex and ongoing legislations affecting most businesses, some of these legal entities have evolved into mini, inward looking conglomerates staffed with all types of 'experts'. I targeted one such firm which had a number of nationwide branches. I met the senior partner in a 'learning' seminar. Subsequently, I met him twice and explored possibilities in reviewing his marketing and organisational structure. That was four years ago and nothing had materialised yet. Possible reasons might be political, ego related and opposition from the other partners (i.e. strong personalities) etc. In my last contact with him, he claimed to have embarked on the 'pruning' route and had made reasonable progress in marketing. However, I have some leads currently on a number of such firms backed up by limited 'insider' knowledge. As I do not have a legal background and being realistic, I am not too optimistic of getting much more than a look in. However, I may partner with an associate who has experience of banking and quality systems in legal firms to market our services together.

Fairly recently, I took on the challenge of selling to a firm of surveyors. I met the managing director, an active member of a local business community group. It transpired that his firm was apparently run like a fiefdom, ruled by several 'barons', him included. My offer to talk to each baron individually was, according to him, rejected by his fellow barons – probably they might have seen it before and were happy with their status quo! How can you convince such 'has beens' that you are different from the earlier candidates in the 'beauty parades'? However, there was still a glimmer of possibility – helping them with sales and in marketing their firm's services. My last update was that this firm had merged, resulting in a new managing director, who has not shown interest.

I would normally target the 'top man or woman' – a proven tactic for getting hold of the 'key' decision maker. On this occasion, I had made efforts to tap into an Asian airline via its sales manager. We had an interesting first meeting in an Asian, networking function. In a subsequent meeting at his relatively spartan office, he was keen for some structured training/coaching for the key, local people. Alas, bad luck intervened when his immediate superior fell ill, which resulted in the latter working only a few hours a week. Despite having made phone contacts with him for over five times by then, my contact had so far failed to bring up the topic with his superior. Sensing the futility of this approach, I decided to bite the bullet and go directly to the top person. The latter, a CEO, was a European, who expressed some interest but no likely action yet for several months. Well, it might have to depend on my persistence plus a modicum of luck in the future.

Since then, my initial contact has now resigned and 'moved on' into oblivion. I am just wondering why. The succeeding CEO did not have a need but quite typically said 'we are keeping your services application and if any possibility comes in the future we will revert to you'. Again, nothing may materialise for months, even years...or ever!

One particular group, which is a real paradox, falls into this difficult category too. It is not about industries per se but more about the specific job categories of people. I specifically mean people occupying the personnel or HR type roles. As what you may term as professionals, they like to be perceived as 'honest' brokers. They are also regarded as the 'meat' in the middle of most organisations. However, a strong limitation is that they often do not have the all-important, overriding authority to decide. In many cases, people here are, bluntly put, 'have-beens'; those who had spent their time in other subordinate type roles and have worked up the hierarchy. One reason for their presence was their valued, supportive type expertise; acting like superglue for the other rough diamonds. Trying to assist the company or its leadership in terms of maximising efficiency, minimal costs; they are normally keen to build good/trusting personal relationships with the lower echelons. Normally playing second fiddle to those in the top hierarchical levels, they need to blend in conveniently with the direction rather than take the initiative. Rocking the boat or admitting ignorance within their specialist field is obviously not their preferred option. Worse still, there may be a strong inclination too, not to show up their own personal incompetence by admitting the slightest inability to achieve any HR related objectives on their own unaided.

Unfortunately, in over 85% of such cases, when they have been my first contact points, no project has resulted. Another possibility is that they may well have their own preferred consultants, i.e. 'mates' built from their years of networking within previous personal HR pool or networks. Overall, they might be perceived by their bosses to be ineffective if they were to ask for external assistance. After all, they might be regarded as experts in all issues (especially in small businesses), even in those remotely related to personnel. It would also be easy for me to stereotype them with such characteristic traits as being flexible (i.e. unassertive), open and team-oriented. After all, HR is often seen as second-tier management, and is normally absent from small boards. The fact that secretaries, half-trained or qualified persons, sometimes assume HR duties speaks volumes.

Any references?

I will end this chapter by dealing with the subject of providing references. To me, this can be a fairly complex subject or even obstacle, which can emerge as an issue on occasions. If my contact was not a referral from a client, there could be doubts in the minds of my prospects about me and my associates. However, these doubts can generally emerge if I have not 'sold' myself well in the first instance. As one client remarked, I might well be a 'fly boy'!

So, how do I normally respond to a request for references? My normal response is to show them my big file of written comments or testimonials from my clients, hitherto collected over the years. This is a pragmatic solution since many ex-clients will have moved on or their companies will have been gobbled up in mergers etc. This action would satisfy most of my prospects that are reasonable and not make unrealistic demands unnecessarily.

However, there is a tiny minority of highly sceptical prospects who must speak to my clients. There are two main categories to this. I will be glad to provide references for prospects to contact provided the latter have provisionally approved my proposals. Hence, the last stage is for them to feel reassured by my references, hopefully confirming my competences etc. as being satisfactory and acceptable.

The other category belongs to prospects who must speak to my clients even before considering any proposal. They seem to think that it would be pointless going further talking about proposals if my references were negative about me. It is normally against my company policy to provide references at this stage for several reasons. First, I never like my clients to be bothered unnecessarily by 'time wasters' who have no intention of buying. I also doubt if anyone would give a 'bad' reference which could be disastrous to someone's reputation and thus affect his livelihood. Can you imagine my clients being bothered by countless prospects, bearing in mind that I would have at least one appointment a week? Personally, I might well find it a real bind if I were in the shoes of someone's client. Secondly, I would never consciously ask my clients to sell on my behalf unless they had volunteered to do so. It is my personal duty and professional role to sell effectively to prospects. From experience, people who are difficult to convince or who may feel vulnerable or find it difficult to trust others, may themselves be fairly untrustworthy. These are likely to take tons of effort and information to convert and convince. With my huge database of prospects, I will tend to avoid giving references too prematurely.

There was one interesting experience, which illustrates the above well. I met the managing director of a business solutions provider at his modern office located somewhere south of London. He was fairly new in his role and had recently started to market his products and services. There seemed to be several aspects of his business that he might need help in. However, at the end of our meeting, he requested I give him three references. Unfortunately, my file of written comments could not satisfy his need to check me out and he must also hear, not just read. Normally I would have rejected his request and walked away since there was not even talk of a proposal. To bother my clients for the sake of establishing my style would never be justified. However, he confirmed his interest for future help, probably in five months' time when he would review his plans. As a compromise, I did supply a reference for him to contact. My gut feel was that this could again be a favour, generously given by my client for another probable pie in the sky!

Chapter 3   Second Meetings and Beyond

As a follow up to the first meeting, these second meetings are normally intended to gather further information or to discuss possible proposals for projects. There would usually be indications of serious interest on the prospect's part at this stage. Who, in his right mind, would want to waste precious time in talking otherwise? Perhaps he needs the company of fairly scarce stimulating conversations, as confirmed in our first meeting. Or, he is too cowardly to say 'No' even at this stage instead of continuing the conversation. But these are also times when the prospects may have second thoughts on the implications of employing a consultant. It could be a question of pride or about what his staff might think of him, possibly regarding him as a failure in their eyes? Logically speaking, the second meeting is one step nearer to clinching a deal.

Some fellow consultants have become involved with 'beauty parades', where they 'parade' their brains amongst and against other contenders. I suspect that this mostly happens to biggish firms, who are spoilt by the choice of apparent over-supply and are thus victims of sophisticated marketing. It is probably a tactic that they themselves are subject to by their customers. Fortunately, I only have to display my firm's attractiveness under such conditions, on a handful of occasions. It could be a demotivating experience if you always have to face a one in five probability of winning. There is always the option of withdrawing your interest. But an unduly pessimistic consultant will probably find it difficult to succeed in consulting!

Some timewasters

However, I can think of one case of a real timewaster (he knew of my opinion of him), based somewhere in Hampshire, who had been trying hard to expand his territory by selling different beverages and drinks related supplies. He had a strongly expressed interest in improving his managers' competences so that he would, hopefully, be free to pursue his other interests. He is not alone in this ambition. Many bosses realise that life is short too. Virtually every appointment with him was postponed when I rang up on the appointed day to check. On one occasion, he had even tried to sneak in through the back way of his factory, when I was waiting at the front reception. He could not possibly have failed to notice my presence since my car was clearly parked in the front. Eventually, he avoided my phone calls after I had invested time on designing a cost-effective proposal which would have met his expressed needs very nicely. Reflecting back, there had been some negative indications. In my earlier two visits there, I did notice that his staff did not seem a happy lot. Staff turnover was high amidst a tough and 'ruthless' working regime. He was one of the very few who financially penalise his staff for being off sick. I can think of two possible reasons for his odd behaviour since he was the obvious key decision maker. Either he had decided to save his pennies or felt that he wanted to remain supreme and was not be too happy accepting any advice to change or improve. Wallowing in one's status quo can well be extremely comfortable.

One timewaster (a printer/packager off A1 motorway) decided that, although my presentation was very good, they would always have problems and other priorities. His 'maybe' answer ended up as a 'not for the moment – keep in touch' outcome. But for how long, I wonder. Being quite a small outfit, I have decided to invest my efforts elsewhere and relegated him to the bottom of my contact list.

I courted the managing director of an engineering design company in 1997. He belonged to the category of the elusive types. My second meeting was with him and his financial man. I did not get far because of his supposedly budgetary issues. I persisted, and made more calls to the managing director. But I still could not get to the bottom of why there were these delays. Frankly, any business relationship has to be based on mutual trust and honesty, both of which seemed somewhat lacking on this occasion. So, I took a brave step and had decided to speak to the top man in the company, the chairman. Not surprisingly, I did not get very far with him either. Not to my complete surprise, the managing director reacted negatively to my move, which I did acknowledge as probably somewhat unconventional. My final decision was to leave them alone and move onto other more open and sincere firms. My usual ploy would normally be to make contact again after the departure of this managing director. It is a case of who would literally 'last longer' – him or I, I wonder?

In a similar vein, this managing director (barrier manufacturer) agreed to my spending a day in his management meeting, followed by discussion of my proposal. By accident, I managed to introduce myself by phone to his chief executive one day. The latter may have objected to using my services for reasons I don't know. This managing director also became quite evasive when I approached him later. Thinking back, he was keen for me to spend my time with his managers but was probably not as keen when I started broaching the subject of my 'paid' involvement. There is one less thing for me to do now: he is no longer on my list for Xmas cards.

Another example involves a firm of just below 100 staff, composed mainly of scientific consultants. Having met the managing director on separate occasions, it was time to meet the rest of the board. There were obvious tensions and unhealthy conflicts concerning the choice of strategic direction amongst the directors. So I was not too surprised that the minority (involving a non-executive director) rejected my proposal after I had presented it to the board. This was the case of weak leadership at the top and the lack of experience/know-how on the managing director's part. The managing director admitted his embarrassment then since he was sincerely seeking help. Initially, this ended with me offering the managing director 1:1 coaching to remedy his weaknesses. And once I had proven my worth, other projects subsequently materialised. With increased confidence, they have now steadily grown in size. Hopefully, he will remain one of my clients for some time to come. Strictly speaking, this was a total timewaster.

A family business (in the cleaning business) located just off the A1 motorway was one of the first companies with which I made contact. The father (was managing director, now semi retired as chairman) saw me first and I was subsequently introduced to him and his senior manager. Unfortunately, it was a case of using my 'free' audit to help them decide on a number of internal initiatives. I am quite certain that it was another case of the prospect getting something for nothing – a fairly common, 'unethical', entrepreneurial tactic. Although we are still on relatively friendly terms, a recent meeting with his son, the current managing director, had yielded nothing.

One lighting company, family owned and just north of London was contacted, firstly via the sales director and then his brother, the general manager. The chairman and proprietor was their father. Their uncle was also involved in the business. Their problems included a 2% profit margin, suffering from a sales plateau and there were ingrained negative attitudes amongst their staff. The GM was keen for me to look at productivity and costs reductions. Somehow, nothing materialised from my approach. But I somehow suspected that the two senior directors were resisting the proposed changes or had already engaged outside help.

'Meet the buyers'?

'Meet the buyers' has been a fairly successful business model whereby a commercial organisation arranges potential buyers to meet a range of interested sellers. This normally occurs over a period of a day at a specific venue. The sellers might be have in common a location, industry type or future project. The organisation probably earns a fee for its commissioned role. Each seller is allocated around 15 minutes or so 'to sell' to or to find out as much as possible from their targeted prospects. To fully exploit your investment, you should come early on the day to network, be prepared for the short appointments and hover around for 'chance' meetings with other sellers who might be available. On the occasions when I have participated, I have managed to meet a large number of potential buyers. Although I did make some contacts, nothing solid has materialised yet. I can identify several main shortcomings associated with this type of business marketing.

Many of the same buyers reappear every year with only a few new buyer companies. This might be due to the sector or location. Unless you wish to renew relationships or acquaintances, it may be unproductive from a business perspective. A minority of the buyers fail to turn up and this might prove rather disappointing to the sellers. Some sellers go over their allocated appointment time limits, thereby leaving less time for the subsequent sellers to discuss their wares and services. The cost to each attendee (i.e. seller) is not cheap since there is no written guarantee of acquiring any new business. Some buyers are quite specific or narrow in their immediate requirements and expectations of the sellers. Some buyers are not always open or accessible to every interested seller as there are unilateral restrictions. Some (especially the 'juniors') are not knowledgeable enough about their own companies' requirements as their bosses are not normally around. Normally, the representatives are predominantly professional buyers by job function, not managing directors or CEOs, who could make authoritative decisions. In terms of networking, the majority of the sellers are from fairly large companies and hence they may not be as open to approaches by smaller suppliers.

It was in a 'meet the buyers' event that the managing director of a local, well-established engineering pump related company showed very strong interest. A proposal to help with sales/marketing activities of this company was produced at a subsequent meeting. The managing director's or owner's right hand man approved it but the managing director had still not approved it yet after an incredible eight months! I wondered who might not be revealing the whole truth in this case. It was plausible that the managing director might not have seen my proposal. Since he was normally engaged in his leisure activities, it had proved almost impossible for me to check with him directly. Objectively speaking, the state of the physical assets of this company was in much need of updating since some of their furniture should have been thrown into the skip years ago. It was like walking into a 1940s film set!

Other interesting prospects

Fortunately, many prospects have been more honest and understanding than the worst ones mentioned in the above examples. In some cases, they were obviously not being straightforward. Many did become my clients. It takes all types to make up this world, and I suspect that some of my meetings have been with a few fly-by-nights.

There was a company which sold point-of-sale materials in what I would term as low value and in a highly competitive market. The managing director was the owner's son-in-law; hence logically speaking, he was in a good, authoritative position. Their needs were to make major improvements in many areas, including sales, productivity and profits – so basically a refocus on its survival. I presented my proposal to the managing director and his financial controller. To achieve such a critical objective in several weeks in 2000, spending just £13k would have been good value for money. Unfortunately, the situation was looked at purely in terms of their cash flow. However, the managing director did benefit from one coaching session. Sadly, the company went into liquidation within a year after I had first made contact. Was it a case of misjudging the seriousness of the situation by the management? It did seem a great a waste of an established company.

Talking of waste, one well-established dry cleaning machinery business in the South went under due to poor strategic direction and high overheads. From my understanding, it was supposedly burdened with customers who were 'not willing to pay'. It was a second-generation business, where the father had started the company but the son, whom I met, had assumed much control in the final stages. I offered to look into their critical areas but my help was declined. A chat with my local dry cleaning company who uses their machines revealed some of that company's weaknesses. The latter included poor after sales service, incompetence and arrogance. I wonder whether it was a case of purposely winding down the business or plain ignorance about other possibilities. My personal opinion was that of a company that had put on a very brave face despite their serious problems. Presumably, closing the business brought the owners some undisclosed benefits.

I felt optimistic when asked to quote a project to help a multimillion-pound business in the medical components business. It had many sites throughout the UK but it was gradually becoming less profitable. There were problematic issues within marketing, people and communications, and the director wanted help in products and productivity. Even as the managing director, he could not explain clearly how we could move to the next stage of helping him! Needless to say, it ended up with no action since the managing director himself kept going round in circles, becoming increasingly muddled in his apparent confusion.

My first 'bloody' presentation and client

Let me share with you one of my first sales presentations. It also resulted in acquiring my first client. I was somewhat fortunate to receive some short but sharp training using the traditional paper flip charts. Since then, I have made very good use of these for many years. On my second visit to present to the chairman and financial director of a film processing company, something unique and unexpected happened. I literally gave them copious amounts of my own blood! Whilst going through my flip chart with the essential vim and enthusiasm, I accidentally cut my finger on a sharp edge of my brand new metal flip chart stand. This was unpredicted and I became an involuntary victim of poor product finishing (poorly deburred product). Blood flowed profusely onto my flip chart, quickly soaking my handkerchief. This induced some excitement in my two-person audience. It did have a good ending. My proposal was accepted the next day. I am also pleased to say that this 'bleeding' experience has never recurred since. But I now wisely carry plasters in my attaché case, just in case history repeats itself.

Other successes

I met the female managing director in the cartographic business years ago. Subsequent agreed meetings were postponed with the main reason given as being non urgent. Years later, I found out that she was now a part time director and she had clearly indicated that the new boss (her successor) would not need my services. As all good salesmen should do – they should continue to pursue any tepid lead till the latter becomes cold – I made contact again, this time with the new boss. Surprise, surprise, the latter has now become my client.

I have had mixed successes with an established pharmaceutical company, based not far from North London. The managing director was amiable but fairly focused and inflexible. In my opinion, he had never seemed to be in 100% control. He would say that so and so was in charge of the 'coaching' side now. Or, he might pass the decision-making responsibility of our topic to his chairman. Despite these complications, I did coach a temporary protégé of his for a number of sessions. Sadly, but not totally surprising, this high flyer then left to do her own thing. Also, after my initial contact, the managing director himself left to become a consultant! I have maintained contact with the new managing director but his main attitudes are about resolving his own problems in-house as much as possible. His birth date (see Chapter 7) would suggest his innate ambition, with a strong, inherent need for control and thrift.

I was fortunate to help a fellow London Business School graduate, who was managing director of an industrial market leader in South London. It was a fairly well run company but one plagued by typical engineering traditions. I was advised

116

that the preferred method was involvement and that suggestions of change should ideally come from the management (i.e. not the managing director). The board accepted my proposal, somewhat reluctantly, I observed. It was a case of receiving some cost-effective advice to help them along the way. I did succeed, except that the 'presentation' of my results was seen as 'poor' (?). Reflecting further on the remark, I highlighted the autocratic style of a investor director because of his 'rule by fear' approach, but he denied it. I hoped that the message would get through and good improvements be made. They still remember my efforts and I am merely biding my time for a management change.

I had success with a traditional furniture manufacturing business, whose parent company manufactured beds. This client had been under severe competitive pressures to perform even though this company was one of the few to operate profitably. My brief was to train their senior/middle managers to become more capable in their all-round management skills. As usual, they were mainly promoted from the shop floor up, hence typical of many British managers, who had zero formal management education. I am pleased to say that my proposal's aims were achieved as promised, with some managers becoming 'fired up' at work, after using my advice. It was a success due to the frankness of the three directors and their willingness to invest in their people. The directors did benefit from some 'feedback' about themselves, their set up and personal approaches. I could have helped them more in other ways but there were severe budgetary constraints. In this case, it was a case of accepting their own diagnosis and offering to meet their specific wants within their limited budget.

Reasons for not buying

Several other furniture businesses, which I contacted, failed to result in any business. My conclusions were that they tended to do their own thing, i.e. be self-sufficient, believing that no you else can possibly help and would apparently prefer to languish in the perpetually 'survival' mode. It is a fact that firms making or distributing the usual common furniture such as chairs are omnipresent ('two a penny') with little differentiation. However, I met a specialist distributor and small-scale chair manufacturer who claimed to do well because of its (perceived) high quality products – the result of being shrewd in outsourcing.

In some cases, the apparent decision maker is interested in 'doing something'. Something negative probably has occurred between our first meeting and our subsequent chat. It would be impractical, though fascinating for me, to eavesdrop every management meeting or discussion subsequently. For example, he might have failed to sell his ideas upwards, sideways or downwards, including to his board members. Some of the many reasons given will include:

> 'It is the wrong time'
> 'There are many things going on'
> 'Company is being reorganised or restructured'
> 'We need to let the dust settle first from current changes'
> 'Doing much of it ourselves'
> 'I am no longer involved, see....'
> 'Let's talk again in the new/budget year'
> 'We are so busy at the moment and the best thing is....'
> 'We will muddle on for the next few months'
> 'I have not decided on any project but may use you in.....'
> 'It is too early yet to decide'
> 'My father (managing director) or directors or chief executive are not interested due to... '
> 'Other priorities have cropped up'
> 'I am interested but so and so is not'
> 'I will need to discuss this with....first'
> 'I will include that in our next management or Board meeting'
> 'We can't afford it now but keep in touch..'
> 'I will need more time to think about it'

'Let's wait till... before I will decide'
'We have decided to use somebody else, e.g. an existing consultant'
'It is at the back burners'
'It's water under the bridge after all this time'
'Company was sold or taken over and new owners would now decide'
'Things have improved since our meeting, so....'
'We can't use external consultants ref HQ instructions or constraints (excuses?)'
'Part of it is being done; need to wait for outcomes to evaluate'
'We have used a consultant since.... for....
'Let us think about this.....call me back to check'
'Things had been bad...can't afford....'

If you are persistent, there will always be 'good' replies that can be used to handle the above objections effectively. Sometimes it is worth doing that rather than letting things rest for a while till the next possible opportunity emerges. On some occasions, it is definitely worth pursuing any slight possibility since you have invested the efforts. You might also have made much progress with your prospect and it would be a shame to just give up then.

Scandinavian companies such as Volvo are known for their teamwork and consensus way of working etc. I shall now describe a good example of such management approach. My brief first meeting with the VP of this South London Company (maritime equipment) led to a subsequent meeting in which I presented to him my proposal. However, he felt that I should also present this proposal to his management team. All went well and my proposal was accepted for action. A few weeks into my preparation, I learnt that the VP had changed his mind. And what was the reason for this? His management team had now apparently got cold feet over what I might discover! Despite an initial dispute over the agreement, I did get paid for the time I used for my partial efforts.

Another unusual variant concerns the quoted price. The managing director of an aerospace company invited me back to present my proposal to his management team. There were five in his team. To cut the story short, their reason for not proceeding was an ownership change, thus making it impossible to use outside expertise, I was told. But my perception was different. I should explain. At the end of that presentation, one of the directors came out with me to have a peek at my car then, a small Nissan Micra. My deduction was that I could only afford to drive a small car because my fee was probably deemed comparatively low. So, they might be wondering whether my success or failure could be accurately reflected in the type of car I drive. Perhaps I am not that status conscious and frankly speaking, I am only interested in delivering a good, high quality job. I did subsequently upgrade my car in anticipation of similar prejudices in future.

Some details about this company might make interesting reading. The managing director, like most clients, made clear that he would expect a customised approach, and that, although it might imply a more costly exercise, 'money would not be critical'. He also hinted that there would be stiff opposition to external inputs. He clearly expressed his keenness to stay on to improve the first phase and to set the rules in the next 'growth phase'.

Again, I did suspect that they had probably not told me the whole truth. Since then, I have always wondered too. This might have been the catalyst for me to increase my fee rate to higher levels. Unfortunately, it seems a common perception amongst some consumers of consultancy that effectiveness is proportionately linked to price. Prospective clients may wish to note: my current levels are nowhere near the exorbitant rates charged by relatively inexperienced juniors from the big hitters.

Unethical practices

You may be slightly surprised to hear that plagiarising does go on within companies. This means that the prospects run away with ideas which I have proposed in our meetings. To rub salt into the wound, they might even pass the work to their favoured consultant or existing coach.

I remembered vividly this happening in a British based, large industrial seal manufacturer, west of London. It concerned the case of a human resources director insisting that his current contact be used. My contact point, the director there, behaved rather sheepishly when this happened. To me it was bad since he had expressed his serious intention to use my services. Moreover, I had invested a day onsite, making observations of his management team, and then spent more time offsite to build up my proposal, specifically to help him. By sheer coincidence, he had moved to one of my clients as their new managing director.

I approached a firm in the paper processing/converting industry. The managing director/owner was fairly successful except for various internal weaknesses, in the areas of leadership, conflicts, complacency and succession issues. It seemed like a 'cat and mouse' game after discussing my proposal with him – he did not want my suggestions to reach his people. His main reasons (excuses?) were that he was keeping busy with his own programme of activities and change. There was no doubt at all that my two sessions with him had helped him focus his mind better. Was it another case of grabbing all you can get at others' expense?

A similar case occurred with a logistics firm which had moved from East London to the Midlands. The managing director was basically interested in TQM, which I offered in my proposal. He and his directors enjoyed my presentation on that subject and had benefited from the knowledge. Sad to say, I have not heard from them since. Another established plastics component manufacturer also enjoyed the same benefit, but at least the managing director partially repaid me by agreeing to be one of my references in my application to become a Chartered Engineer of the IMechE.

A third case involved a small distributor of technical equipment in South London. The managing director was keen to survey his customers, asked me for a proposal but insisted on seeing the sample questions too. One of my associates assisted me with the questions but she did warn me of possible plagiarising by this firm. She was right on this occasion as she had seen this happening many times before. This managing director did decide to do the survey himself but to what degree of success? That also meant one action, which I am free to take – a reduction from my list of people for future Xmas cards.

One other interesting example involved a Finnish company in the electronics display industry. The managing director had an MBA too. He seemed quite open when discussing his perceptions of his corporate issues and challenges. I could have written a short chapter about that meeting. His main objectives were to reduce staff, be aware of the cost of sales and to increase profit margins.

He also claimed to know what he wanted. But he narrowed down his priorities or requirements to basically instil a realistic culture of non-wishful thinking and to deliver as promised (to customers). One of my associates, a psychotherapist, accompanied me to present our proposal. According to him, our role was to deal with 'mindsets' and issues not covered by his TQM programme. He also had a firm figure regarding what he would like to pay us! Regretfully, they eventually decided to use another firm for TQM and plodded on in-house, no doubt, using some of our ideas. To be fair, he did say 'no promises' at some stage of our contact. These two words have been uttered on many occasions and have quite often led to nothing. Perhaps, these are signals to shut up, close my case and walk out! For me, it might also be a lesson in which I learnt about how one particular Finn works. This was a rather rare example of my exposure to this culture and I would not like to generalise too much. Subsequent contact with this Finnish company had yielded nothing. Possibly, the whole management team was purposely recruited so because they were 'clones' of a particular management culture.

Interesting but tough prospects and fees

Sometimes, prospects would show great interest in my services. Naturally, I would reciprocate by investing in my time and best efforts. A good example was a Cambridge (UK) based scientific firm, which distributed laboratory apparatus. The managing director wanted me to quote for some management development work for his managers. However, when I presented him with my proposal, he seemed visibly shocked, and deemed it expensive and unacceptable! I was surprised too, as I had been upfront telling him my typical fee rates, which were competitive. Perhaps he was one of those who does not listen. However, he has now retired and I hope to interest his successor instead. So far, the latter has decided not to respond! Perhaps he had his orders, and he also remembered?

A similar decision ended (my decision) my selling relationship of a few years with an equipment hire company based in West London. The story here was slightly different. The managing director was a marketer, who, like me, was also a member of the CIM. However, his problems were related to organisational/structural issues. Somehow, he could not be persuaded of how valuable an external expert could be in effecting the improvements which he so desperately needed.

I believe that my fee was a real stumbling block. Sometimes I am amazed at how little some people are prepared to pay to enhance the performance capabilities of their people, who can be instrumental in boosting their bottom lines.

There was this opposite case of a small instrument firm based in the northern Home Counties, run by two partners. The main partner had expressed strong interest in what I could achieve for his company at our first meeting. He even appreciated the Xmas card calendar I had sent him. However, his other partner was strongly against our ideas and had become rather sceptical about wanting to make the improvements. In his cynical eyes, my proposal was too cost effective, i.e. too cheap! Indeed, another important lesson in pricing. Subsequently, I learnt that the son of the 'friendlier' partner has now joined the business...am now wondering what he's like. I did speak to this son but his first reactions were 'to do things in-house'.

There have been second meetings where a few people were supposed to be present. On a number of occasions, even the managing director (my original contact) was absent. I have concluded that this was one good sign that the earlier strong interest was probably now absent or diminished somewhat. They were initially present, possibly as a way of showing *some* courtesy or respect. Perhaps it was curiosity that I managed to arouse.

It has always been my policy to pursue as far as I can once I have made the contact. In some cases, I have met more than two managing directors of the prospect firm over the years. One situation concerned a laundry business which focused on linen and related items used mainly by hotels and restaurants. The first managing director I met was keen on implementing various process efficiency improvements and improving his managerial competencies. Not long after my second meeting with him, I discovered that he had left for greener pastures, probably having been fired. My teleconference with the chairman/owner did not materialise into anything positive as he sounded rather evasive. I suspected that he belonged to the group who prefer internal actions by their own employees. A few years later, I was in contact with it's the company's new general manager (GM operations), and they now have a new managing director in the new structure. Meetings were held with the GM but so far, this has resulted in nothing. Could it be that the chairman is still wielding his strongly negative influence behind the scene?

Productive endings

I will end this chapter with more examples with productive endings, i.e. where my offer to help was accepted. Many became happy clients of mine and have added to my long and varied list of successfully completed projects. Some of their comments were listed in Chapter 4. Below is just a selection.

An electrical design and manufacturing firm (since taken over) had a managing director who subscribed to the Jehovah Witness philosophies. Initially, he was wary of my influence in his company in terms of planting 'seeds of ideas' within his people's minds. His sales director managed to persuade him to give my skills a try. There were some organisational and sales issues which could benefit from impartial analyses. The exercise I did (including interviewing in my car due to their space shortage) was regarded as being 'objective and very useful'.

A packaging company run by a three-member family did have a positive ending. It started when I met the son in a business setting. The father (the managing director) then agreed to see me to explore possibilities. The second meeting involved presenting to the father, his son and their financial manager. The meeting ended with the managing director labelling me as a 'fly boy' (wished I could fly as well). He also voiced his scepticism and claimed to have the skill of predicting personalities from the shoes people wore! Nevertheless, I did get the order and spent several months effecting change (working mainly on skills and modifying the ingrained traditional attitudes). On reflection, it was one of the most rewarding of client relationships that I have had that I enjoyed. Many lunchtime breaks were spent alone in the local friendly village pub eating my scampi salads in rather tranquil surroundings. The son has now assumed the managing director's mantle and it might be time for a revisit soon to check up on things. As far as I am aware, they are still holding their own amongst the competition.

There is an interesting sequel to the above client. I am now helping the son in to increase sales amidst an environment of weak selling competencies internally. This will be a real challenge since the managing director has different philosophies from his deceased father, who founded the company. Also, there are several products involved in a number of market segments which makes targeted marketing almost impossible.

One videoconferencing company in Bucks became a client when the marketing director desired some 1:1 coaching for him. The main motivation was his lack of management training, which he believed had adversely affected his overall performance. My proposal was approved instantly by him in our second meeting. As in many cases, a fairly large number of managers have succeeded, based on their own innate merits but have lacked good exposure to external ideas and skills. According to my records, he was amongst the few clients to reward me full marks on my client's evaluation sheet. He was soon promoted to managing director, a gratifying success story in my books.

A British subsidiary of an Asian/Pacific parent was keen for me to stimulate thinking on issues regarding planning, strategies, problem solving, and organisational structure. These were conducted in a number of workshops, including brainstorming offsite. We ended up with a very long list of issues and a wide range of realistic solutions, which were appropriate for the company. Needless to say, the managing director was rewarded with a more senior role and is now engaged in ambitious plans for expansions in the future.

A company involved with geographic data software was keen for me to manage his workshop on conflicts, future strategies, relationships with their parent company etc. It occurred as planned with some interesting comments being elicited from the participants. Unfortunately, for my client, the managing director was an inevitable victim of some restructuring plans initiated by his Europe based HQ. Occasionally, I do see his ex-company's van roving round updating their cartographic data.

Main concerns of companies

It will be interesting reading for many to see the concerns which prospects have mentioned over the years. These have been mentioned in many of the discussions I have had. The majority have come from the initial meetings with prospects, who generally open up and 'offload' their challenges. On close scrutiny, you would find some similarities or themes of problematic areas. The companies involved are not specifically identified here but they obviously share much common ground with varied business or management areas. Generally, due to the lack of time at these initial meetings, it was often impractical to probe deeper for further details. Normally the details (e.g. causes) on these symptoms would have been obtained when they become my clients. These comments could give very useful clues as to what really concerned the prospects. In effect, real awareness of the issues mentioned could be a good, quick substitute for having to go through the same learning curve of at least 20 years. Some of these concerns or needs can be used as good material for a separate book. However, for the moment, a line of bullet points (mainly verbatim) is given for each company that I have come across and spoken to:-

Little control over price sensitivity, sensitive (to consultants) by workforce.

Lacks money, slack controls, at crossroads (strategies), succession, structure, motivation.

Morale and people issues, changes, lacking knowledge.

Sales and team ineffectiveness.

Get people to recognise 'continuous improvement', business lacks discipline/procedures and mismatch with Germany's (another subsidiary) results.

Increase revenue; restructure sales team, internal sales project management.

Difficult to bring *kaizen* into offices, improve order to despatch process.

Small expensive batches (due to use of manual adjustments), management succession.

Big product range, large stocks and long lead times.

Improve fire-fighting mode in sales administration.

Bad impression left with customers due to poor reliability.

Need for good quality people.

Expensive supplier, poor market penetration and lack of inputs by key people.

Complacency, managing director without authority, vast product range, sales person left.

Imperfect fit of people to roles, sales people not empowered, poor product design.

Increase sales, increase team spirit, realignment of resources to the target markets.

Growing pains, unpredictable (demand) distribution of products.

Calibre of the younger generation (sons), conflicts.

Cyclical market, to implement cultural changes.

Underachievement in sales, need market focus.

Been reactive, need to increase customer base and cash flow.

Competitive environment, complex documentation, lack of urgency and focus.

Efficiency issues, big wage bill, high customers' standards, resource allocations in shops.

Weak technical leader, assembly is not core competence,

Service standards, specialised products.

Apathy of staff, prevalent sickness.

Not done much for the future, not enough training for senior managers.

Cultural change: engineering is frightened of change,

Bureaucratic processes, managers not deputising, misunderstood priorities, long lead times.

Survival – lost a big client.

Hitting sales target, know what to do but need to execute actions faster.

Imperfect organisational structure, how to pitch business, low conversion ratios.

Need to include others, teambuilding, structure.

To capture and standardise internal knowledge for use throughout the various branches.

Must have more work.

Not feel that they are moving fast enough.

High churn of orders, lack of orders, projects cancelled, feast and famine syndrome, people struggling at deep end.

Development needs but managing director is uninterested and headstrong.

No critical mass, parent went bust, workforce is not cost conscious, irresponsible managers.

Resistance to change but change is needed to survive.

Training and succession, business portfolio, lack of central resources.

Cannot plan, no plan, poor structure, disheartened workforce due to pressure, low productivity.

Deficient management – needs training, excess inventory.

Not ideal operations and organisational structures, poor interface between commercial and technical, inherited many.

Plateau on sales.

Improve process flow in car repair business.

Different divisions, different perceptions/priorities, lack of understanding of customers.

Lost money in UK, smaller turnover, smaller margin, restructuring cost.

Difficult to increase price, room for improvement in internal communications and structure.

Increasing competition (from GEC, Ferranti), direction driven from US, not a quality product.

Rapid change in technology (software), no confidence to invest, not safe or clear market.

Staff – no loyalty, never been led and had done their own thing, much fire fighting.

Customer services dept reactive, not proactive, bottom people talking badly about top people.

Difficult to analyse past performance, can't organise BS5750, site services draining on resources, relies on auditors, information not out quickly enough, more management techniques needed.

Not easy to sell; wrong pricing, to keep up the turnover, relying on goodwill of other organisations and users.

Some negative feelings, need to merge and to invest, build up capital.

Warehouse is running out of space, slow speed to market place, competitors are everywhere, no worldwide sales and marketing strategies.

Main issue: how to get the strategic decision making and thinking into the 'blood'?

Unsure of marketing strategy on how to attack, no end to product development.

Lacks relationships with the commercial and technical sectors, no standards, hence need for testing.

Keen on staff morale, sales important.

Relationships with customers, scope to increase sales, need profits but margins might be squeezed.

Performance standard on supply chain, need to increase manufacturing base here.

Increasing paperwork, lower value activities, strength of £.

Factory issues: reducing efficiency, poor production manager, to find trading partner overseas.

Issues with quality and systems, problems might be missed if too busy and engrossed.

Cost reductions within projects.

Need to increase growth in new field but under resourced, time management.

Integration of Italian and British cultures re: manufacturing and sales/marketing.

Long lead times, low margins, update product ranges, achieved below budget, cost cutting.

Find resellers, fast expansion, no resource to target, not brilliant in sales/marketing.

Very labour intensive, three expensive departments.

Increase sales and profit by reducing costs, stock and increasing margins.

Sell, reduce costs/outgoings, difficult to motivate.

Too many strategies – need to tidy up, need to work on coal face of NHS.

Reactive re: sales; service manager confused about requirements.

Cost and time to market of products, high pressure to perform, in difficult markets.

Bad debts stop expansion.

Difficult to help because he is in high tech and not being able to find the right companies.

Main market is decreasing, some staff are redundant.

No exposure to business, not function as a team, reluctant to accept direction, been here long.

Key people are badly equipped, apathy of new people, cost pressures, complacency.

Lost four top sales people in one year.

Negative effect of strong £ on exports.

Shrinking maintenance market, no culture of repairing, Rolls Royce mentality.

Low margin site, low motivation/morale, sales do not listen; major clients are upset, appalling communications, disillusioned attitudes.

Very negative attitudes, unstable product, whole sales force left.

Traditional functional barriers, personality conflicts, lack of real life awareness.

Chaotic manufacturing, unable to predict, need to reduce inventory.

Need to acquire French company, increase new channels, work overload, handling of customer queries, reactive procedures.

Unsuccessful product launch, budget used up for marketing,

Very serious people issues, was autocratically led, no career development, long lead times.

Structure, operational procedures, reliant on knowledge of a few individuals.

Commercial structure and processes, unreasonable parent company, poor systems integration.

Be more competitive, break into other markets, not innovative.

Traditional culture, monitor action plans, need to motivate, support sales, be competitive.

Not enough sales, low conversion ratios, new computer system, weak customer service.

R & D into production, sales/production interface, managing director needs more skills, delivery performance.

Short-term sales forecasting, insufficient data, dependent on third parties, need confidence in framework, laws needed for processes.

Not cost effective delivery processes, relationships with head office, arguments with customers.

Large number of projects, ideas for *kaizen*, traditional mentality of workforce, priorities using SPC.

High workload, need products quicker, much fire fighting, need more *right* people.

Not cohesive structure, growing pains, reporting procedures.

Lacks image in UK, difficult to sell, low motivation.

Wrong people in wrong jobs, change from technical driven to market focus, needs buy-in of own people.

Lack of slick business procedures and discipline, lacks management development and time, not much marketing.

'Clay layer' in the middle between directors and junior staff, company processes, staff attitudes.

Strategy is unfocused and does not have enough details, communications.

Not dynamic sales, inefficient transport, lacking discipline, customer service affected.

Strategies for keeping or selling products.

Need to survive (personally), fear factor, very tight situation.

Relies on technologist and marketing department, venture capitalist wants sales trebled.

Volatile cellular output, large product variety, lacking people, low volume/high cost, high lead time.

Reducing economies of scale, variable quality of management, costs, succession planning.

Growing too fast and changing circumstances, leading to staff turnover, including directors.

Poor US management, problem with sub contractors, poor quality of technical staff.

Processes not streamlined and inefficient, inconsistent work flow.

Autocratic leadership, weak sales team, 'always done it this way', weak ownership of problems, poor productivity, motivation and low morale.

Question marks over the calibres of sales people.

Lack of sales related measures and project management.

Difficult to plan, redundancies due to downtown, now lean and mean.

Improve sales, structural change, inefficient processes.

Challenge from new technology to his publishing business.

Relatively young board, inflexible services, too much democracy, quality issues, conflicts.

Negative company image, risk averse mentality, weak market definition, inflexible procedures, high costs.

Organisation between individuals, project managers are not taking key strategic decision.

Fragmentation of business processes, lacks vision, fear exists, *kaizen* message needed.

Very competitive in supplying government, high labour cost, conservative, tied up with Danish.

Antiquated sales: waiting for phone to ring, inefficient factory, slack, low productivity.

Reduce lead times, lower costs and inventory, and increase customer satisfaction.

Inadequate structure, increase distribution outlets, lacks creativity.

Not profitable enough, need to establish core business, going through change, sell more.

Negative attitudes, poor customer service attitudes, to change culture.

Manufacturing – process flow, costs.

'Weak' sales team, poor motivation, traditional ('always done it this way'), ownership of problems (decisions taken by others).

Conflicts at top, to increase profile and deliver on time of accounting services.

Insufficient resource, too engineering focused, wrong people in wrong jobs.

Family owned, no investment, emotional and headless chicken syndrome.

Need to justify projects, difficult to control some projects and be more commercially aware.

Reactive, query handling by customer service, work overload and distracted by subsidiaries.

Weak technology, unprofitable, not reacted and be more market focused

Weak structure, lacking operational procedures, reliant on a few individuals, lacks good decisions.

Ex managing director took away product development, long training period, overworked, poor delegation.

Poor quotes handling, need to market research and develop you product.

Good with existing customers but weak in new ways (not innovative).

Poor priority management, difficult to maintain timescales, managing new pressures (processes, IT), more support to sales, be more technically competitive.

Fallen demand for blow moulds, some redundancies, poor work flow, not as a team.

Ex managing director was dictatorial, weak exposure to business, inexperienced, weak teamwork, insecurity.

Wrong structure, changing customers' needs, team building between sales and service, conflicts due to personalities/change/priorities.

Difficult selling, structure needs improving, disgruntled employees, variable qualities of teams.

Insufficient time, family and cultural concerns, teamwork and sales issues.

High loss of top sales people.

Very challenging technology, need to reorganise sales and management, weak strategies.

Strong £ affects exports.

Appalling man management/presentation, limited motivation, sales support not listens.

To increase turnover via price hikes and lower costs.

Insufficient sales and improve customer service.

Incapable managers, weak communications, improve things to reduce wastes.

Interface between sales and production, right products on time, skills development.

Need external 'change catalyst'.

Define objectives, clear strategies and teambuilding.

Selling skills,

Sales and motivation issues.

Overheads, speed of reaction, conflicts.

Integrating the material control system.

Disjointed operations, low volume of high variety, after sales problems, complex strategies.

Too small an organisation, sales management.

Not achieving input/investment, effects of recession, lacks management skills.

Finding better distributors and recruiting agents.

Expanding overseas through agents, lacks sales/marketing skills, production problems.

Poor attitudes, low profits, low sales, uncompetitive.

Sales force (long in tooth) and not slick, narrow product range.

Poor time management, failed to do certain things, need to update manual, restricted capital.

No system to cope with marketing, workshop not functioning properly, not very profitable.

Motivate shop floor, sell more, and control costs.

Lacks planning skills, variable attitudes, poor problem solving.

Traditional (middle management), weak selling, reduce costs and people.

Product development, international marketing plan, no network of agents.

Sales/marketing problems (1 product line), knowledge of competitors, managing proposals.

Them and us, shop floor barrier due to stable workforce.

Imperfect computerised marketing system.

Morale and people issues (recruiting, cope with few people – thinly manned).

Structure – to identify good middle managers and motivation.

'Traditional' middle management, need to reduce costs and people, disappointing sales.

To develop new products, no agents network, poorly run marketing.

Lacks PR/market intelligence, small margins, people issues, lacks competencies.

Contracting market place, more glass companies (competitors).

Aged workforce, shortage of skills, outdated sales literature, people untrained, weak market intelligence, big loss.

Big customer, lacks confidence and sales techniques (engineering services)

Weak strategic direction, not good (capabilities) people in services, selling abilities.

Selling, product development, marketing.

IT business system, people issues, integrating businesses (maritime business).

Reactive selling, service manager is confused about requirements, falling sales and profits.

Deciding on which markets to be in.

High pressure to perform continually, cost and time to market, where to spend money.

To increase market share but designer is lazy, not widen knowledge and likes the familiar.

Bad debt, looming recession from US.

Since in high tech, difficult to find the right companies to sell to.

Put business plans into action in Europe, some arrogant people.

Fire fighting, dissatisfied client base, no market research, not made transition from R & D to selling.

Poor marketing strategy, unsure profit margins, underselling, no salesman.

Not proactive enough, quality specification varies (hand finished).

Lacks financial resources, spent much in product development/mould tools, inefficient, quality issue, lacks time, new facility, lacks enthusiasm.

No middle layer, need contract management, not produce products fast enough.

Poor closing, low motivation, poor attitudes in factory.

Lacking self-confidence, many errors made, chips on shoulder.

Strategic direction, investment in machinery, continuity of company.

Growing pains, no strategic input from parent company, too close to issues.

Recession, cultural gap with Chinese market, products sourcing, direction, strategic planning.

Low morale, unrealistic cost targets, lacks direction, reactive.

Quality issues, barriers between management, non experts in production, costs, inefficiencies.

Pricing, distributors, clash of products, planning. recruitment, marketing plans.

Better production flow, bad communication, labour intensive.

Payments from overseas, profitability, effectiveness.

Not comprehensive quality manual, lacks capital, too cheap, lacks staff, no sales manager.

Recession, cost effective production, more sales, merging two units into one.

High price, lacks team spirit, lost orders, conflicts at top.

Very young company, loss situation, no investment, needs more sales, uncertain market.

Need strategy, light on management skills, drop in sales over years, ineffective sales force.

Poor marketing efforts, needs cash, liquidated client.

Need volume of work in capital goods area, much time spent recruiting sales manager.

Complacency, not enough 'measures', hard to cost accounts, resistance to change, expensive.

Very specialised product, poor sales levels, very expensive compared to ordinary vice.

Future directions (strategy), plateau sales, going backwards.

Few managers, need to be more efficient, no official buyer, wears several hats, under-utilised computer system.

Bad debts (poor credit control), low profile, low margins.

Weak manufacturing/IT systems, cash flow problems restrict expansion, limited accounts.

Consolidating manufacturing operations, easing out poor sales performers.

Manage growth and grow profitably.

Recession has hit sales, lacks capital.

Needs good people, commercial manager – overstretched and tired, sales director – weak interpersonal skills.

Not profitable and higher absenteeism.

Large set up costs, not very profitable; no one understands his son's vision.

No capital/reserves, large loss, little sales, management change meant 'less relaxed', internal conflicts, unclear marketing strategy.

No sales training, no financial reports.

Need large multinational companies, lacks investment in equipment, no products, very price competitive, high overheads, slow to react.

Disappointing sales director, static sales, shortage of skilled people, high costs.

Operational issues, capacity of UK manufactures, reliance on food wholesalers.

Only one sales person, restricted to contacts, limited time.

Team building, long manufacturing lead times, rejects, high material and labour costs.

Printing market collapsed, high costs, increase product range, no ability to develop staff.

Forecast sales, order processing, market planning.

No plan/strategy, no internal communication.

Monitoring sales people, critique corporate strategy.

Low sales and profits, low labour productivity, temperamental sons.

No fixed price, low conversion ratio, difficult to define/claim quality, ineffective internal personnel.

Internal organisation, bad planning, weak procedures, poor morale. annoying attitudes.

Very price competitive, limited premises, has bad debt.

No job contracts and job descriptions, under pressure, poor time management, can't delegate, internal conflicts, cultural issues.

Affected by recession, room for improvements.

Ineffective coverage by distributors, no marketing, lack sales staff.

Increase sales, some negative attitudes, lacks direction.

Improve productivity, reduce costs.

Sales and marketing issues.

Difficult to sell and achieve JIT, looking for replacement, survival mode.

Non threatening type coaching needed for two individuals.

No strategic plan, no written procedures, find new markets, useless MRP.

Fear of recession, customers reducing stock.

Slightly disorganised, not overstaffed, lacks space, need to heighten profile.

Lack ability to seek service markets, no sales training, limited to UK customers.

Appalling state, losing money, poor trading, bad account management, lacks good technical service, resistance to change.

Severe communication problem, no marketing, unprofitable sales growth.

Narrow product base, dependent on house building industry, most products solvent based, complaints on product development.

Bad trading, poor profits, not maximising use of CNC machines, no time planning.

To expand customer base.

Drop in sales, high price.

Reluctance to change, identifying big UK customers for new product areas, accurate costing.

Dropping sales, expensive products, high cost of sales, low margins, high stock levels.

Ideas for launching new products, market research and more effective selling.

Adding new product to current portfolio.

Tough competition, expensive, low profitability, structurally weak.

Implement sales initiatives more aggressively, sales management and motivation.

Implementing change successfully and to survive the internal politics.

Not good quality product, average operations, visible 'wastes'.

Weak in managing and delivering change programme, i.e. the buy-in processes from marketing to operations/delivery.

Finding good quality sales people and technical problems on IT products.

Market is getting tougher in terms of customer service, keeping costs down using the right marketing/distribution strategies.

Replacement of the managing director and sales manager.

No product (subcontracting services), not forward thinking, attitudes issue, managing director failed to sack, lacks practical training for skills.

Small relative to competitor, poor management, difficult to communicate, fits and starts in delivery due to supplier, lack people skills to retain and attract.

No overall strategy, only one sales person on the road, power culture of managing director, who makes every decision.

No corporate plan, dilemma over size – to maintain size or expand further.

Project times not well controlled and problems would cause catching up difficult, weak staff loyalty, antiquated machinery, high gearing, and unclear strategic options.

Underperforming directors, lack line managers to manage motivation, multi sites (e.g. three buildings affecting communications), need to be World Class with performance measures, overdue plans.

Weak communications and manufacturing not handled since dependent on others.

Traditional products/methods, static sales, high costs due to high labour intensive activities, many were grown up with the company.

Lack understanding, tolerance of peers' behaviours and understanding of a manager's role, conflicts between technical and sales.

Investment thinly spread, individuals in grey area/wrong jobs, needs planning and strategy.

Weak communications, was autocratic/Victorian, weak managers in provinces, poor adaptability, blinkered views at HQ, poor stock control, narrow focused.

Lack of trust, conflicts, meetings not open enough, weak in hiring.

Seeking other links/agency, increasing product range, focus on being specialist.

Despondency due to not winning enough or won jobs of poor state, quality too high, better – hence higher prices, no specialised marketing.

Very short order book – reacting to needs (i.e. reactive), sales executive not fulfilling sales role, need to have plan and not want any listless chickens.

Chairman felt difficulty accepting changes, nobody criticises him, difficult to distinguish personal and business issues, poor attitudes and motivation amongst managers, soft and susceptible managing director (chairman's daughter), lacking in direction.

Consolidating two offices, need support from BT, increasing rent, not wealthy, unsatisfactory auditors.

Flexibility of production process, low level of retainable sales (customers were supermarkets), image of production and delivery due to change, hard to set Scanlon type bonus scheme, price sensitive markets, thrive on chaos.

Sales (recession), reducing margins, stronger European competition, need reorganising working methods in printing pre-made section.

Weak financial control of costs, low productivity, weak planning and routing for processes, lax control over documents, job times, slow response to changes, owners were good engineers not managers, high sickness levels and turnover.

Need help to facilitate internal discussions, improve external communications, middle tier of management needed, cash flow issues, increase fire in the belly, no right hand person, and low concept of good management practices.

Team building needed, UK managing director had blind spots, took 12 months and confronted people, UK was biggest risk, no marketing urgency (re: US VP).

Planning changes giving bad impression to customers, too much stock, need high plant utilisation, first line supervisors weak intellectually.

Problem with design and manufacturing, poor profit mix in order book, tired staff, reactive, jobbing environment, need to reduce work in progress and stock.

Organisational chart, part drawings, layouts.

Tension between sales and production, weak in delivery, less professional image.

Hit by recession, few big eggs, expensive, needs more customers, laid back attitudes, low profit.

Workforce – long in tooth, not slick sales office, tired product range, poor yield and quality, poor marketing performance, to increase market share.

Not enough time for each customer, weakest link in administration.

Low profit, technical training, no marketing system, needs purchasing role, cannot see ahead, image issue, workshop manager not coping, problems hidden from managing director.

Hurt by recession, cannot plan, struggle to breakeven, high costs, shop floor needs motivating.

Inefficient selling, quality problems (25% returns), quality of information, 25% deliveries on time, poor morale, bad absenteeism, highly negative attitudes, weak financial situation.

Lacks planning skills, not always successful in tackling problems, variable people attitudes.

Weak middle management, disappointed sales, need to reduce costs and people.

Inefficient layout and processes, needs market research, managing director dislikes feedback.

Limited resources, hence lean and mean, need to develop products, no network of agents internationally, no marketing expertise – poorly run.

Only one product line that has sales/marketing problems, lack awareness of competition, TV industry suffering recession, cut wages and overtime, static price, very competitive, no planning possible, two big eggs (60% of revenues) in basket, cash shortage.

Cannot stand still, three or four years behind, stable workforce is a barrier inhibiting progress, them and us mentality.

Inadequate computer system and sales/marketing software.

Operating relationship with Norwegian parent, sales growth and morale issues.

Lacking good manufacturing organisation and capital from distribution, overcapacity, limited demand, product too expensive, price sensitive, reliance on NHS, heavy discounting, costly to give quality repair, slow rate of change.

Lack personnel, low leadership, no systems, too much interest in technology, need to respond to special customers, confused by MBO.

Need to increase sales, improve attitudes and motivation.

Poor relationships within his team, to grow market faster and be innovative.

Need quality control checks, ignorance amongst Taiwanese owners, unskilled and untrained staff.

Weak communicating, marketing weak professionally, manufacturing can be improved, human and personality areas not working properly, image worsening, wrong specifications or bad understanding, weak control over 'waste', weak in purchasing.

To double sales, need to be more hard nosed and improve.

Lacking focus, not enough post sales customer development, careless in administrations (shipping errors), external perception needs improving,

Questionable goals and strategies, compulsory redundancies.

To reduce manufacturing cost base, implement changes in design, foundry and transport.

Too many managers, favourite systems, limited working capital and stock holding, try to be innovative, people were feather bedded.

Disastrous appointments (not thought through), risky marketing strategy, very slow decision making, hurt and frightened by change, hard to achieve leadership/expert position, not listened to customers well.

No marketing dept, demotivating due to loose structure, volatile sales director, long serving staff resisting change, excessive wheeling and dealing overseas, non dynamic finance director, them and us, measuring performance, late deliveries, low margins.

Delay in products and design, weak manufacturing organisation, declining competitiveness in price and technology.

Scarce field support engineers, small company with high risk, products difficult to use, undisciplined environment amongst engineers, people left due to pressures.

Lacking direction, not getting enough quotes, laid back towards laziness, mediocre image, suggestion scheme (not working), below 70% productivity, very low profit, plan for future succession.

Over engineers products, not know enough from research, not fully understand customer requirements, delivery, people assessments needed.

Highly complex paper system, much and rapid change recently, need fresh blood, not enough time, people using their brawn not brains.

Top heavy administration (13 sets of paper), losing paperwork, to increase work, poor customer communications, low profits, customer service issues, historic constraints.

Low turnover and profit, unfocused marketing.

Swedish headquarters not convinced of Basingstoke's site, Swedish pride and arrogance, need to build team's confidence (personalities).

Increase business through greater effectiveness, recruit new people, team working.

Funding lacking from the Ministry of Defence, poor quality of publicity material, imperfect things.

Loathe to change, speed of change, how anticipate market.

Friction between departments, let down by suppliers, availability of products, suppliers not vetted, inefficient order picking.

Square pegs in round holes, need understanding of strengths, fears, aspirations and weaknesses, strategic review, problematic relationship with US headquarters.

Very tired managing director (on crutches!), unclear future options, blunt, controlling wife/partner.

Not enough sales staff, low turnover, low margins, disappointment in employees.

Conflicts, attitudes issues, imperfect structure, people numbers.

Hectic, tremendous growth, cannot grow faster – hindered by cash flow and conservative US headquarters, infrastructure.

Increase product range, 'tired' managing director, capital injection.

Too much democracy versus much discipline, errors in manufacturing, quality issues, scrap, rework, many processes.

Strong bakery culture, project management not taking key strategic decisions, how best to organise individuals.

Fragmentation of business processes, quality issues, bad interfacing, people fearful, overstock, much idle time, lacking vision.

High labour cost products, aiming for paperless system.

Antiquated selling, poor quality of people, managing director not trusting, inefficient factory, lack of urgency, very poor communications, inflexible image.

Worthless cold calling.

Delivery, costs, communications between manufacturing and sales, lack of customer knowledge, wearing too many hats, too reliant on certain industries.

Inadequate structure – too much on managing director, conservative stock policies.

Confidence problem within management, sales training.

To establish core business, need to sell more, cash shortage.

Quality and robustness of software, product to market.

Issues with people's attitudes, culture and company philosophies.

Get message across, engineering frightened of change, sales force not actually selling, cost reduction, standardisation needed.

Integrate computer systems, losses, compulsory redundancies, low margins, inefficiencies, high overheads, overpaid, weak forecasting, too many people, much stock, old designs, too wide customer base, insufficient marketing, poor quality from Yugoslavia, high returns.

Problems with everything, low profits or loss, dropping revenues, lost good salesman, not excellent quality, bad communications, low morale.

People discipline, teething problems with computers, lack of time, quality and delivery issues, teamwork.

To increase sales force, professionalism lacking in sales, capital industries quiet, employees stay too long, too much overhead, unproductive and expensive financial controller, seat of pants operations, managing director too involved.

Lacking proper delegation, worsening customer loyalty, dropping quality, high overheads, motivational problem.

Direction, costs not controlled and monitored, capital stretched, low morale due to strong trade union.

Recession, serious competition, cut throat, overproduction, very small margins, lack sales training, no marketing strategy, side tracked, lack professionalism in project handling.

Lacking resources, reducing headcount, 500 chemical variations, acute competition affecting margins, no management judgement, to develop key managers.

Financing machines, capacity problems, strategic choice, narrow spread of customers, high interest rates.

Cannot convince customer the technology and ability to satisfy needs, got alcoholic quality assurance manager, too day to day, laid back management style.

Internal relationship issues – sales and technical, manufacturing and accounts, engineering and production, engineering and sales; needs to be leader and be different, people defensive and not keen to change, too busy to develop.

'Pulling' not great in MRP, to reduce non-added-value, stocks and lead times.

Management team interactions, team building.

Outdated ways, research needed, dropping sales and margins, high set up, losing few accounts, higher material costs.

Fear everywhere, people overstretched, poor people managers, lacking professionalism.

Lots to do, mapping out new organisation, how to move forward and structural systems.

Ensure enough business to sustain, margins to pay for overheads, eliminate 'waste'.

Middle managers not empowered, low morale, poor absenteeism in shop floor, all paper manufacturing system, five months lead times, engineers not very knowledgeable, low productivity.

Improve focus and increase ownership, costs control, increase sales accounts.

Limited resource to develop design systems, issues not well understood or communicated, bad deliveries, not enough new products, dropping profit, lack time.

Senior management's ability to identify weaknesses and give the ability to manage change, have the confidence and energy.

Define objectives, design organisational structure, senior management not working well together – not approachable (personalities).

Too long in merging, thus causing confusion and uncertainty, lacking clarity over 'right' and 'cheapest', define objectives and current issues.

Poor sales forecast, overstock, too many specials, too flexible, not good service or delivery, low shop floor motivation with complacency, not customer focused, weak response.

Small batches, need traceability.

Downturn, IT system too big for company, three weak key managers, low profit, loss of good image, succession planning, slack sales discipline.

To increase throughput, obtain consistently good quality and reduced manufacturing times.

Profit warning, too much scrap, high purchasing costs, supply chain issues, people 'fit', structure.

Reduce throughput times, big batches, low motivations.

Over sophisticated costing, low volume but high value work, different standards needed, low profit contribution, long machine dwell times.

High cost base, high lead times, improve manufacturing, big gulf in morale between office and shop floor, too much variety and specials (cannot rationalise), high set up costs, heavy reliance on foremen.

Weak in administration, managers not multi purpose, some managers – poor value for money, mature product lines, not using liquidity well.

Late deliveries, shortages of standard parts, unrealistic promises, inflexible machines, increasing costs, few bottlenecks, blinkered designers, shop floor people paid to work and not think, lack of people, difficult to forecast, people shortage.

Finished goods stock and work in progress, low gross margins, lacking new products, long lead times, suggestion scheme not working, and lack in communication.

Product development plan, poorly equipped shop floor on machine tools, weak in South-East Asia, large product varieties, high shortages, large set up costs, need manufacturing strategy.

No one able to quantify the challenges and manage the change programme.

Tougher market, importance of customer service, issues of costs, marketing and distribution strategies.

Sales orders for medium and long term in a mature industry, to increase profits as operating (material, gas, electricity) costs increase.

Inefficient processes in operations and software development, weak monitoring tools in operations/delivery, poor quality, much wastes and missing problems.

Speed of training and time needed in learning to sell.

Frustrating not winning the right sort of work (reason – inconsistency?), lacking awareness of causes – commercial terms, price or engineering.

Need to reduce operating energy costs and improve efficiency in foundry.

Need geographic strategy quickly, management capacity.

Limited resources, no big marketing budget, need be more focused, small marine science market, higher customer expectations (reliability, quality software) and becoming more discerning.

A quick glance of the above concerns reveals clearly that they do fall into several broad but distinct categories. Many prospects would probably identify themselves with these too.

Lacking structure, poor sales skills, constraints on growth due to skills shortage, lacking time, competitors (fast and efficient).

Need to outsource aluminium die castings overseas for cost reasons.

Less than 10% quote to order conversion, weak in sales and marketing, micro business.

Weak in recruitment process, training of new employees/management.

Lacking man management, growth restricted by cost (capacity issue), imperfect service (sales and marketing not integrated), lacking branding, several cans of worms.

Very ambitious growth plans, recruitment issues (skills lacking, retention), supply chain inefficiencies, fuzzy brand image.

Some attitudes problem, conflicts at professional level, just above average on productivity, high level of rework.

Restructure to globally source, relocate manufacturing bases overseas and coordinate global activities.

To reduce risks, simplify the business, introduce cost controls, antiquated fragmented IT system, many people late in their career, traditional and different attitudes.

Fire fighting against official plans, poor time management, ineffective sales, poor management styles.

Not achieved sales, got leads (wrong focus?) before quote processes.

Bringing structure together, increase sales and profits, training issues, ability to plan.

Staff retention, weak management competences, to increase sales, motivation issues, lacking professionalism and direction,

New vision and expectations (change at the top), sales need remotivation, better, more efficient service.

Recruitment, insufficient sales, improve financial systems and attract external finance.

Bigger targets, to keep up momentum and think outside square.

Capacity issue, grow business, set up, optimise and selection of new plant/equipment.

Complex products to produce, developing new markets and new products, increase sales, weak project management, fire fighting, people skills.

Non-aggressive marketing approach, customer complaints on installation and times, be more commercial and remain as market leader.

Incompetent business partner (cousin), dropping sales and profits, many customer complaints, losing customers, lack of sales, serious internal conflicts.

Traditional engineering company, very small, try to get into new markets, not enough time.

Weak marketing, fearful/suspicious culture, labour intensive, lacking time.

Price sensitive, tiny company, lacking knowledge, negligible sales efforts, low conversion, autocratic Middle Eastern boss, unfocused efforts.

Autocratic boss, no real managers, overpaid salesmen, some bad debts, no sales data, poor implementation, lack market intelligence.

Bottleneck in design office, errors, lack project management, poor interface with factory, imperfect structure, poor information flow, too many changes, heavy reporting structure.

Indispensable boss, inefficient processes, inexperienced son/Director.

The above one liners can be summarised as follows:-

Sales and marketing (strategies, pricing, investment, methods, skills, agents/distributors, economy)
Customers' related problems (image, segments)
Process efficiencies (equipment), systems (IT etc) and operational efficiency
Structure, organisation, functions and size
Leadership, motivation, management, functional skills and competences
Profitability, financial investment, cash flow and costs/overheads
Cultural issues, behavioural, attitudes, work practices, motivation and communications
Strategies, direction, focus, conflicts and team work
Change management, mergers and related processes
Product and service related (quality, stocking, innovation, standard, delivery)

Other specific opportunities can come from the 'pain' suffered or having the urge to improve:

- There exists internal ignorance of serious 'survival' problems, which were later made known to me.

- Some awareness of the current issue(s), but internally, the client may not fully recognise the symptoms, lacks the know-how to define clear-cut objectives and act appropriately.

- Ambitions exist to remain 'top dog' but would be keen to find out the what, how etc.

- Need to improve specifics, as defined by the client or needed help to define better what these are and be offered the justifications (ROI) for actions .

- The current timing is 'right' (e.g. structural refinement or make over necessary before selling off) or pressurised by the venture capitalist/investor to exit soon.

- The effects of Internal conflicts or perceived problems that are no longer bearable. Examples are the serious internal haemorrhage of the firm and issues that are severely limiting future progress in one or more areas.

The above pages should offer invaluable insights to the range of real-life business problems faced by commercial organisations. Any consultant worth his salt should seize on the above survey as warm tips on what they could focus on in their own marketing and selling stages. It will, of course, depend on his areas of expertise or choice of comfort zones to operate in.

Potential clients may take comfort in the fact that they are definitely not alone if they are suffering from similar concerns. What is surprising is that, despite the seriousness of certain concerns, no action was apparently taken to rectify the situations. Some of the quotes were from clients, who have subsequently benefited from our interventions.

Chapter 4   Types of Prospects and Clients

Almost 100% of my prospects and clients are in the commercial sector. Like most businesses, they consider themselves to be in highly competitive markets where only the best could probably survive long term. Hence, it has not been a total surprise for me to meet a whole range of unusual or unexpected behavioural patterns, and much of that is shaped historically by the cultures they are in. Cultures are, by definition, formed by the inmates of their respective institutions and are often the causes for various symptoms.

The public sector has always appeared to me rather impenetrable and full of seemingly 'apathetic' management, who are in cloud cuckoo land. You only have to look at the government of the day for clues. People in this sector seem perpetually bogged down by bureaucracy. Going on special courses to learn the tricks on how to acquire these clients may be a solution but that could mean joining the many hopefuls with the same desires. Somehow, the mere thought of helping these people often substantially deflate my own motivational levels in view of the rumoured bureaucratic hurdles that I expect to encounter. This is definitely a situation which can be difficult to perform your best.

It can be useful fun to classify the prospects and clients into distinct categories. In the very least, they can now categorise themselves and see where they fit in. It is not always possible to be very definitive as each one may well have some aspects of other categories. Thus, I have given and invented some appropriate names for those I have actually met whilst executing my proposals or at my various stages of contact. For clients who happen to be reading this book, my congratulations if you can recognise yourself amongst these. My descriptions are not meant to be derogatory or disrespectful. I am just being frank, as I have always aimed to be – to convey clearly my honest perceptions. Some may find varying suitable combinations of truths or descriptions from these categories. Also, do remember to give yourself a big pat on the back if you happen to fall into more than two categories. These categories are by no means exhaustive or complimentary. There is no 'buttering' of any kind involved here. You are described according to how you appeared and behaved – no more, no less. You may indeed, wish to add a few more yourselves.

Quite a few prospects belong to the Friendlies category. Their chief objective is not to offend anyone even if they are strongly pushed into the other direction. They were typically nice people; many of them well educated, qualified and fairly smoothened around the edges (i.e. balanced). Invariably, they would smile, appeared very welcoming from the first second of our meeting till the very end. With their characteristic frankness and relaxed composures, they would generally share several of their thoughts and concerns. However, their niceness would normally mean one thing – their strong need or natural preference to involve and consult others in the decision process. They would not dream of upsetting anybody even if they feel that they are right. Obviously, the main difficulty here is that it will not be easy to act assertively upon meeting such people. They have treated you nicely, and that does not necessarily mean that they will automatically become your client.

On many occasions, much time had been wasted subsequently, in pursuing the long chain of discussions. This could carry on *ad infinitum* until a time when the earlier (potentially problematic) circumstances could have improved or changed, so that the situation would no longer become favourable to me. An example involved the managing director of a baby foods manufacturer who had told me in our first meeting that their management system would be changed. This subsequently meant his relocation to a far away place, and his replacement by a new managing director, who unfortunately, already had his own advisers.

I would put the owner of an importer/distributor of a tiny business in the above category. He imported low cost rubber products from Asia and resold these to European wholesalers. In his middle age, he did not seem overly ambitious, merely contented to maintain his million pound or so annual turnover. After a few minutes' of initial discussion, it soon became apparent that he would not become an immediate client, and probably never will. He was the 'plodding' type and any improvements made could well upset his current leisurely paced lifestyle too much. However, he suggested that I might offer to help to his ex-partner (a competitor!) and also to call on his Asian business neighbour, located next door in that business park. Being a 'typical' Asian businessman, unsurprisingly, his neighbour was fairly content to do his own thing.

Another example involved a small business supplying bar type equipment. The managing director confessed (honest of him to do so) that he did not know it all but that the timing was not ideal. Continual restructuring in his attempts to contain overhead costs seemed paramount. There were issues of process inefficiencies and he was also holding joint venture talks then. He would be classed as a 'tepid' prospect with a little potential; someone confined to a relatively low priority.

One client of mine is obviously a Friendly. It took him 3 long years and a takeover bid to convince the one or two toughies in his Board to wake up to the realities of the situation. Always approachable, he is always extremely polite and considerate in all his actions and words. My coaching session for him, which included assertiveness as a topic, did teach him something though.

Timewasters could easily form the largest category in anyone's books. It might seem rather sad for me to say that I would put many of my fellow academic colleagues in this category. For obvious reasons, some people will call them 'tyre kickers'; contributing significantly to my car mileage and so-called carbon foot print. They could certainly boost up your costs especially if each tyre costs over a hundred quid. Some would feel obliged to see you as a matter of a routine part of business activity – a 'what's out there' mentality, which is fine. Perhaps, it was a useful way to appear as a 'busy boss' by filling up their diaries. The few who offered me between 5 to 15 minutes were obviously not showing any modicum of seriousness in their intentions. Others were 'pressurised' into a meeting because their bosses told them to meet me. These meetings tended to be fruitless because of their fairly low commitment levels. There were those who would cancel appointments more than once, thus clearly indicating the importance or amount of respect they had given you. Some would promise that they would call you back (common message via the receptionists) but they would never do so or rarely did so. Others would verbally express their interest and would not respond clearly anything of substance in a short time scale.

I will also put in this category, people who have willingly made appointments way in advance (e.g. two or more months ahead). But they might subsequently cancel the appointment the day or week before the date. This applies to an ex-client in electrical engineering whereby his secretary would normally say: 'Sorry to do this to you....'. I can almost hear some of you remark that this is part of normal selling; expecting to be given low priority and thus be treated as such. But, when such cancellations numbered more than three in a row over a few months, I do feel justified to question the seriousness of the other party. I will now highlight a few more poignant real life examples.

In 2005, the financial director of a small and young company (DIY products) phoned me asking me what the agenda was in our proposed meeting with him and his managing director in two days' time. It was supposed to be just an exploratory chat since I had met his managing director about nine months earlier. As predicted, this meeting was cancelled due to it being labelled lower priority, with his promise of calling me next week to chat again. But, this was the third appointment made with this managing director. The earlier dates were seen as either 'too busy' or 'impossible'.

Another example concerned the managing director of an engineering company based in Letchworth. Being fellow Chartered Engineers, we always have had interesting, convivial chats, exchanging information and progress updates. He would ask for proposals on a number of objectives, which he would take months to decide on. On occasions when I did meet him, he had implemented some actions internally, or worse still, had used someone else, on what we had discussed earlier. In the end, feeling a bit like our poor Muggins, I had decided to cut my losses by finding new pastures and not contacting him again.

I courted the managing director of a supplier of temporary, portable accommodation based in the South West. His company had several regional offices all over UK. He was initially keen for me to assess his managers' competencies and be interested in receiving some feedback on him. So the whole project was agreed and he had confirmed the go ahead with his CEO too. The latter had labelled it as inexpensive; an encouraging sign. I had also confirmed our agreement with him verbally several times over a period of months. Just a week before the first series of interviews of the project were to begin, I phoned up to check. The receptionist told me that he was busy (normally a negative signal of something amiss here) and that the project was off! I was meant to have received a letter from him a few weeks earlier, around Xmas 2004! I did not receive such a letter and had been wondering if it had actually been sent or had even been written. The receptionist promised me a faxed copy, which I did receive later on the same day. It turned out that some internal changes had caused the postponement, which could still mean that a resurrection was possible in future. It would have been a different and interesting type of project where I could travel round the country, enjoying some scenic views as a perk at the same time. After three years of 'courting', I was told that there would be a management buy out by the managing director and his senior people. This time I did not revise my country-wide schedule as I half expected another 'not ready' reply. The sale had taken longer to transact than he first estimated. As to be expected, the managing director was now virtually not contactable since his mobile seemed to be perpetually switched off. Phoning his office would always bring a negative reply. Leaving a message was also a waste of time. The first negative indication about this character came when he admitted that his managers had not been told about the agreed programme, even though he had confirmed verbally to me otherwise on earlier occasions! Another apt description for this managing director would be extremely deviousness or lacking integrity for this example. This could well be the case when maximum time had been wasted.

One slightly unusual example concerned a youngish managing director whose father was the chairman in a bus/coach related supply and repair business. Being based in the eastern side of London, near the River Thames meant a fairly long trek across central London. The first meeting went well before one Xmas since I was asked to make contact in the New Year, possibly helping in some coaching, recruitment and value analysis to reduce his component costs. Many phone calls later had still not yielded another meeting. My contact would ask me to call him at a future specific time in his office when I would manage to speak to him on his mobile. The main problem was that he did not carry his diary with him; hence the apparent need for him to check his future movements at his office. He could still be not back in his office as he had predicted due to delays in getting back. Or, even if he was in, he might be busy and would pass on the message that he would call me back. Did he ever call? You have guessed it. He never even called back once despite his several promises. Would he have forgotten, even when he had noted down my phone details? Frankly speaking, I would assume not. Unfortunately for him, I doubt if he, as the boss, was well respected internally, probably due to his poor attitudes towards people. He might not even fully realise that his actions had incurred time costs on both my side and his people's. I am still hoping (only a minuscule hope) that the penny will drop one day and he will become my next client.

Another kind would see me but they would proudly and vehemently declare that there were no negatives within their companies. I call them the Okayers. These would offer me a long list of actions, which they had taken or about to take, and the resulting or expected, positive outcomes. In some cases, they would also justify to me their decisions – quite an interesting move since I was a total stranger to them! It was totally plausible that these companies had really no obvious issues, unless they were putting on their brave faces. To me, the silver lining in these cases would be to 'learn' something from them by asking a few questions! Why were they particularly successful, and in which area(s), if any? Was it a case of someone wearing rose tinted glasses? I do think that many were not being honest enough to admit imperfections for fear of having to consider using my services. Sometimes, my proof would lie with the comments that some of their staff had confided in me on earlier occasions. For some of them, they were initially, genuinely curious about my wares; hence making the appointment to see me. It is possible that having slept on their concerns, the latter might now appear less threatening. Fortunately, this category had probably formed less than 20% of all the prospects I have contacted.

Pussy-footers were the weak and indecisive. Dithering over decisions, they would have a strong need to confer and look for a consensual outcome. They would be likely to change their minds and forget about any earlier conversations. Time did not seem to matter too much because there could be other tempting 'flavours' of the week for them to try out with the third Joe Bloggs. It was also likely that a slight but growing fear of upsetting important colleagues or subordinates might have crept in here. Members of this category might include those who were nearing their retirement; so why would they want to bother too much in their last leg of an epic corporate journey? Was it energy efficient to rock their precarious water-craft? Hence timing might be a factor. It might be true to say that they would prefer to remain in the background, lying low if possible, rather than appear to be the initiators. Getting commitment from them might well require tons of persistent and persuasive efforts, and definitely patience.

Those who consciously avoid the truth or delay the fulfilment of their obligation would be named the Crooked smilers. There are some distinguishing features from the Pussy-footers. They would put on a disguised form of friendly smile, perhaps consciously trying to appear inscrutable, much akin to the famous Cheshire cat's. Occupying the top of the list would be those who might try not to pay their dues incurred and very occasionally even invoices for work done. Those of you out there should realise that many consultants are pitifully small fry and to them too, positive cash mattered and could be vital for their survival. It should not always be a case of 'do unto others, as you had been done by yourself', probably by the 'bigger' boys. I would also put those who had conveyed an image of near perfection of their firms in this category. No person or company could claim real perfection; there is always room for improvement. It was a case of justification and having to face the reality and sometimes to accept the need for action before it was too late.

I do love the Gratefuls. Presumably, everyone else does. They were the ones who would be fully appreciative of the efforts you had put in; to resolve their problems and probably, even rescued them from probable extinction. These could be the ones who felt the strongest need to recover quickly or to survive. Perhaps, their pain had become rather unbearable. Some clients would fall in this category when they would buy my services again, partly as a means of rewarding me. Familiarity may breed contempt, but it can be utilised to help engender and build a deeper level of understanding within a past client. Sometimes, it was often a case of enforced changes, which would require my somewhat refreshing and objective perspectives to bear on their issues.

A few comments from some of the Gratefuls whom I have had the pleasure of helping:
        'First class all round.'

managing director (teleconferencing)

'...course useful and engaging....'
marketing manager (pharmaceutical supplier)

'A thought-provoking study.'
managing director (telecoms)

'My short personal contact has been worthwhile... key
to success...independent assessment on
relationships, styles....'
Ops director (engineering services)

'It's been extremely worthwhile.'
managing director (medical health care)

'Unconventional but excellent style of Kwan made the
sessions...interesting informative.'
group engineering manager (air conditioning
manufacturers)

'....very intuitive with enormous experience...excellent
value.'
managing director (object software)

'....rating for 'insight'...could mark it excellent.'
managing director (metal finishers)

'Very interesting and useful course.'
ops controller (furniture manufacturer)

'...very professional service...guided company through
a difficult process of change.'
finance director (electrical components)

'Good refresher on management techniques.'
marketing director (telecoms)

'..The study was handled very professionally.'
chairman/managing director (engineering)

'We greatly appreciated the services provided and insight given.'
managing director (software)

'Of great assistance in developing my potential within my company.' director (IT)

'..very useful person to talk with and bounce ideas off...objective from outside.'
sales director (engineering conductors)

'Very thorough exercise....'
managing director (packaging)

' some useful insights into key areas...'
managing director (synthetics manufacturer)

'....most interesting and unusual product......'
managing director (engineering)

'proved cost effective and informative.'
chairman (video/film)

'...solid report.. plenty of discussion points and solutions.'
managing director (scientific instruments)

'I found the sessions extremely useful.'
technical manager (telecoms)

'Very accurate perception and summary of a complex situation – good insight.'
senior VP (software)

' training/guidance useful, comprehensive and thorough.'
ops director (Engineering)

'...success of your coaching programme...remarkable results...more efficient....... positive responses from customers.'

chairman (logistics multinational)

'....I know that the staff involved have found your individual coaching both instructive and confidence building.'
managing director (IT services)

'...we have made some significant steps along our continuous improvement path....like to thank you for your help, assistance and guidance in all these aspects.'
managing director (mechanical engineering)

'Excellent all round; re: quality, value, effectiveness, objectivity, service and competence.'
managing director (security services)

Almost opposite to the Gratefuls were the Forgetfuls. These Forgetfuls will justifiably pocket the benefits of your involvement and not the slightest trace of your input will seemingly be remembered. 'What have you done for us?' might be their typical question when I have made contact with them at a later date. It would be regarded as some form of icing on the cake if clients could recall even the tiniest impact of my intervention. In many cases, the outcomes have become part of their everyday activities and hence their culture.

Skinflints (hopefully self-explanatory) are those who believe that everything can be had for free. Are they not aware that even consultants have to 'eat'.... something? They might impose an unrealistic budget limit or would regard any five-figure investment as expensive, even when compared to their seven-figure turnover. Probably they were non-subscribers to 'you get what you pay for'. My advice to them would be to have another good look at their own personal remuneration against their potential gains from receiving competent external advice. The returns could be immeasurable and might well amount to several times the sums involved. After all, they might have conveniently forgotten that they would not need to pay external advisers for the company car, bonuses, petrol, accommodation, pension, insurances, desk space, secretarial support, phone bills, heating, water, lunches etc.

An excellent example concerns a three-person band selling systems to independent retailers. By firing two employees to cut costs, he managed to bring his company into the black. Unsurprisingly, the main priority was to increase sales. My initial meeting revealed that the managing director was the chief sales person, supported by his fellow Director based in Ireland. There was no doubt that he would need advice to improve his less than 10% conversion rate (i.e. quotes to orders ratio). There was further evidence that the sales processes used were ineffective The ultimate destiny for this struggling micro business was obvious. So my proposal was designed to review and expose their current sales weaknesses, evaluate their sales competences and assess their external market perceptions. Although it was initially priced at the mid four figures, it was considered unaffordable. We then talked of a figure in the low four figures that was deemed the maximum acceptable. We ended up with the managing director himself asking to pay an initial payment of three figures with the balance to be paid, based on performance! I was even asked for references to be spoken to as well, for this pitifully small project.

The Sceptics form a subset of the Timewasters. Forever questioning your logic or asking for evidence and examples, they can be a tough lot to convince. Perhaps they had never had the fortune or experience of using really competent people. I have suspected and have confirmed that a relatively small minority in this category had worked in advisory roles themselves. This could inevitably mean that they should be capable of confidently distinguishing genuine expertise from the omnipresent 'charlatans' (often redundant executives?). Sadly, they might even have experienced failures themselves (victims of their own bad advice). As a result, they might have become quadruply dubious about receiving any external assistance, however genuine and potentially effective that might be.

As many successful bosses have high 'power' needs, it is not surprising that some of them would cling onto and shield their existing empire, fearing that consultants might snatch some of it away. It is also about the need to keep control of every happening or action, lest someone else could sow seeds of dissention amongst their people.

The other cause could be their fear of misplacing their trust in the unproven and unknown. I have come across quite a few accounting or finance people in this category. Anyone who could lay claim on improvements without supporting solid financial data might seem suspect to them. Hey, my aim is not to rob you of your pot of gold, which you have scrimped so hard for or creatively retained, and hidden somewhere within unknown corporate space! To be fair, there have been many horror stories of clients being led up the proverbial garden path by the slick talkers, and fleeced by some 'cowboys' in consulting. It would be nice if they could somehow exude even a whiff of trust, especially when the paths themselves are well laid out and created attractively.

The Eagers could be really desirable to have as your clients. Their enthusiasm to achieve something via some actions could sometimes be overwhelming. On some occasions, they had tried their own ideas and had failed. Having reached this point when they must successfully tackle the issues, they could not be anything else but appear at least 120% eager to proceed. Being unable to decide realistically on what they must focus on could prove to be their main downfall. They might also demand a little miracle, *NOW*! But, I do like them though.

Their main problems would concern others (particularly those with power/authority) who might not share the Eagers' strong interest on improving their companies. There were times when I listened to all their problems but their superior's apathy and the 'wait and see' mentality could spell the end of my involvement. Sometimes, I had to sell 'upwards', which can be very hard going, when venturing into the unknown, organisational labyrinths. They could certainly have my sympathy for the frustrations they might bear. Probably, a change at the top or thereabouts would be very beneficial.

Some people were truly Sweet-bitters, ones who started off well, appearing appreciative of receiving advice and interested but could end up displaying a totally indifferent and opposite attitude. In some cases, I felt like playing the role of an unpaid consultant, who had positioned their jigsaw pieces into position during our exploratory meetings. This meant helping them with sufficient clarity for them to proceed onto the next stage of improvements, problem solving etc.

I had an interesting one-hour meeting with the managing director (and accountant) of an IT company in the wireless business. He poured out surprisingly frank answers to my verbal survey questions. For example, he revealed that his sales director had to be replaced due to her pregnancy and that the turnover amongst his IT developers was very low. This did not really surprise me when he said that the track record of in-house successful products was poor. He must have had quite a high tolerance level for technical underperformance, unless he had the fear of losing his technical resource. Eventually, he got cold feet and suddenly and bluntly saying that I could not possibly add value to his organisation. It was probably an accountant's way of saying that he could not see any increase in his current store of beans. Or was he really a Sweet-bitter?

Another example concerned a small search engine firm in London whereby the relatively young managing director agreed to proceed with rescuing him from his serious issues, subject only to checking my references. The latter were provided in good faith but my subsequent contact with him failed. The common message from him via the receptionist was that he was 'tied up'. He was one of the very few whom I have met over the years that really needed external expertise to sort out his internal conflicts (at high level) etc.

Unfortunately, his earlier poor choices of external helpers did not seem to get him anywhere. He then said that he was too busy trying to set up a US office (would he be able to cope?) and he apologised briefly for this delay. Incidentally, he said that my references were 'quite complimentary'. Well, you can only invest finite efforts to offer genuine help. This may be a case of him having to wait till I have exhausted my warm list of other prospects. Frankly, having been through the above palaver, I don't' care a damn!

I met a director and investor of a servicing/installation agency based south of London. When we first met, he sounded rather grand with his eight office staff and 80 engineers. He seemed keen for a follow-up meeting. Subsequently, he phoned to cancel a meeting. Many attempts were made to contact him. On one occasion, he asked me to phone the day before to confirm our meeting venue near his home but he cut off after answering his mobile, and his office never knew his movements. He had also failed to return my calls despite my having left him several messages. What a Jekyll and Hyde character!

Others in his clan would agree to consider a proposal but could later ring up to express their zero interest. For goodness sake, aren't we are all human? Could it be that their superiors found out from my contact and about my possible involvement and have, unjustifiably said 'No! No!'? But why? There were a few cases where these prospects became almost impossible to contact again at a later date. The sad fact was that they were invariably hiding behind the truth, against their real need or desire for change. They then became another category, which I term the Timids.

These Timids avoid talking again by shielding themselves behind their receptionist or PA. I would get messages of them being in meetings or not being available. These are the people who do not tell you the truth and often give evasive responses. Obviously, such prospects do not even have the courtesy or had a teeny bit of courage just to say 'No, thank you' to your face, ideally giving a succinct reason too. They no doubt have their reasons for not revealing much, especially to a stranger. Possibly a fairly prolonged 'courting' period might work here. If only they could be more upfront, even to the point of embarrassing me, I would not have minded. In fact, they could probably be considered as a subset of Timewasters.

It can be extremely frustrating dealing with those in the category of Half-listeners. These people would be keen to know what might be wrong and how to correct their errors. Unfortunately for them, they had not picked up clearly in our communications what they ought to be doing in terms of priority. They might well be having an internal mental debate, possibly including my additional ideas. From a selling viewpoint, half your explanation could be going in one ear and out the other. Juggling too many balls at one time could well expedite their downfall and having a strong but easily distracted mind would not help them either. It would definitely require much patience and tolerance when dealing with this category of prospects.

Spongers are the true opposites of the Half-listeners. The former would pick up every word you have uttered, thereby maximising their learning and investment. It could be very satisfying indeed, when dealing with these types of clients, knowing that very little would fall on deaf ears. Your efforts have not, apparently, been in vain. On the other hand, you need to be extremely careful in choosing your words when dealing with them. The cynic might say that every piece of comment or evidence had been noted, to be used if a future occasion demanded. You could very obviously see that no syllable had gone astray when talking to them. They would take in everything you say. If they were also endowed with fantastic memories, it could prove to be painfully fatal, should I ever make a slip.

As I have always tried hard to be a conscientious 'trouble-shooter', I never expect to linger or would enjoy lingering on with any client. As many can testify, it is fairly easy to overstay your welcome. From memory, this situation might have only applied to one client, whose ego could not accept my apparent 'taking over' of his company (i.e. his baby). His son had actually remarked that 'the messenger (i.e. me) had been shot'! It is my preferred policy to 'hunt' for new challenging projects rather than coax existing clients for more work. As a shrewd client of mine would comment, I would regard myself more of a hunter than farmer. However, farmers might say that life is far easier and productive in reaping rewards, after good efforts are sown with just a few good clients. Somehow, many of my projects were naturally one-offs; thus consultants would not be needed if everything was hunky dory.

Hence I have this One-offs category. However, I do suspect that there must be more than one need that I can help satisfy amongst those in this category. The only saving grace is that I might be regarded as being a narrow specialist in only one area. This can be a natural assumption amongst bigger clients, who are normally exposed to one trick actors. For smaller businesses, it seems a definite disadvantage to engage a consultant with just one speciality, since they are unlikely to afford hiring several specialists.

The Not-arounds are a funny, if not an exasperating lot to deal with. If I was offsite, away from my prospects, I could not physically see whether the receptionist or PA was telling the truth about someone's whereabouts. My simple conclusions were that, either my target was physically away, really busy 'working' (i.e. 'tied up') or simply avoiding me at all costs (probably through ignorance or fear). Without inside knowledge, situations of the last category would be impossible to confirm. There have been odd occasions when the receptionist has officially passed on my details to my target, with me still hanging on the phone. However, there have been times when the former (in the same room!!) has sometimes been heard to convey a negative response (e.g. 'not in'). In practice, I would fully accept that the really busy, effective people in this category would not be in for at least 60% of the time. Catching them could almost equate to winning a handsome lottery prize. With very few exceptions, my long experience warns that doing business with this category is rather remote.

I enjoy the 'blue-sky' type of work when I am amongst a group that I would term Visionaries. They normally insist on starting from the big picture perspective, which I would be supportive of. But you can only go so far on such a strategic approach before you end up hitting the earth really hard. I have helped these clients in various strategic/problem workshops, usually ending with lists of actions or ideas. At the end, if they were happy with the outcomes; so was I. But it could take some getting used to with these folks. The unfortunate thing seems to me that I might not see the end results or improvements with this type of very short involvement.

The Windies are those who have shown good interest, and who have also talked much more than their fair share in meetings. An alternative good description could be Hot-airs. They make disguised or implied promises, offering you some hope and most of the time, nothing comes of it. There would always be circumstances which prevent the fulfilment of their commitments. Another likely explanation was that these were really sociable and nice people. They had much to tell, at least tell (or offload) someone, who appeared to them as receptive and was also prepared to listen. Presumably, their satisfaction came from impressing their willing audience.

One managing director of a sheet metal company stood out as a friendly example of a Windie. His interest was to talk about his other business ventures and his personal interest in the film and TV industries. He even went as far as agreeing to introduce my daughter onto one of his pet film courses. Now, we (and probably his staff) could probably deduce and understand why his business was not as successful as it could be.

One slightly annoying category I would add would be the Control-freaks. Fortunately for me, I met only a handful in my travels. They would even specify precisely what you must include in your workshop, virtually what words to use and how the processes were to be managed. Sadly, their inbuilt fear of the unknown or unexpected, had inevitably limited the benefits to them. I have often wondered why they had agreed to use someone's expertise under those circumstances. Probably, I had merely to help facilitate the event, with my clients there just to make important observations of the interaction. Perhaps, they would not have the guts to say what they would really have liked to say, do or ask the questions themselves. I was merely acting as their mouthpiece for their varied messages.

Allied to the apprehensiveness of the Control-freaks would be the apparently cautious Dip-toers. This category would just try a little wee project, such as one coaching session for them initially, followed by their evaluation of that and then a decision. The main disadvantage to them (not me) was one of cost effectiveness. In the medium term, they would need to invest proportionally more for the same results by their preferred method of doing one thing at a time – a sequential approach. This method could incur a longer gestation period before the results would be realised. I have always offered a holistic approach where several areas could be looked at simultaneously, aiming to ensure that my client would not miss out on any opportunity now.

Unrelated to a once very famous dotcom company, one category would be the Last-minuters. How many times would I get a last minute call from people to change the appointment or be informed of a change of direction? These were the people who might struggle in prioritising their actions. Perpetual fire fighting seemed to be their norm and they were forever pushing on panic type buttons. It would also include those who would wait, sometimes for obscure reasons, till the last second to decide on my proposals.

The Hard-softs were a sophisticated lot indeed. Their initial attitude of being as 'hard as nails' could apply to their dealings internally or with external suppliers. Somehow, this façade might change quite suddenly to one of being nice, and apparently soft. Thus, making an accurate judgement of them could always be difficult, possibly to their own detriment if we had inadvertently misinterpreted. Could it be that they were naturally nice as pie but putting on a hard exterior would make them feel more secure and protected?

I have met several people whom I would term as old hands in the magical field. I call them the Vanishers. They could disappear literally in seconds in thin air when I phoned. Or they might actually even be out at the appointed time and place when I turned up. Several could not make the appointed times due to sickness or be imposed by an unavoidable event, which I would regard as fairly forgivable. Even then, they could easily have phoned me, with the kindness that was aimed to stop my wasted journey. On the odd occasions I had given at least one real life example above. It would seem an unlikely coincidence that no one else in their company would have known their thereabouts at that time.

Possibly, there was a genuine mistake. However, it could be most annoying at the receiving end, especially when a journey of 100 miles was involved.

On one occasion, this managing director of a US firm in the catering industry was not there. His PA appeared with his diary, showing the crossing off of my appointment. She asked me whether he had confirmed or changed the appointment. Actually, she was the person whom I made it with! Hopefully, I would be lucky the second time. I was indeed lucky next time. As one would have guessed, this might have caused the degree of heightened serious interest as I would have liked.

I have mentioned the Brainpickers or their equivalents somewhere! These were the people who had used the context of my introductory and subsequent meetings to glean as many tasty morsels as possible for their own consumption, gratis. Sometimes, they might wish to gauge (benchmark) their current achievements against what might be possible or the current best practices. Naturally, their main objective was to learn enough for DIY, probably after I had gone. What they probably did not realise was that they would have benefited from an impartial perspective, which could have helped them uncover possible problems and solutions to those problems. Unfortunately for them, the latter could normally be best delivered by external expertise and not navel gazing. OK, they could use someone they already knew but they would still need to face the ethical dimension of exploitation. There have been several occasions when my customised proposals have been used to guide their existing consultants! It would have been interesting to know the final outcomes. Another ploy that had been used was to treat me to a normal lunch and tease out possible tips for their problems. Luckily, I was a victim on only three such occasions. This could also be a ploy they use, whereby their staff would be unaware of my presence. The difficulty is always about making the judgement as to whether this prospect will become a willing client one day!

An outstanding example of this concerned a leading non-red meat producer in Eastern England whom I visited with an associate. We understood the site director's requirements well (we assumed and thought so!). We were asked to help supply leading edge but proven ideas to potentially help update his factory. He had employed other consultants before and eight years ago, had apparently researched the world for new ideas. Our proposal was virtually rejected as it did, according to him, address his requirements well. What transpired was that he had expected us to provide reference sites for him to consider or even visit before deciding to go ahead on our proposal! Ah-ha! Not so fast, since I am definitely not in the business of providing ideas *gratis*! From my 'free' preliminary interviews with his managers, it did seem that his perceptions of his own needs were somewhat incorrect. To be fair, there will always be Brainpickers amongst all of us, hoping to gain without incurring any expense to ourselves.

My final category is labelled the Know-alls. This should be self-explanatory. They are very similar to the Okayers. This was a rather annoying category of people, who would naturally almost want to do my projects for me (if I allow them quarter of a chance)! A few I spoke to on the phone even jokingly informed me their daily rates for being *my* consultant! Again, even someone with years of good, solid experience within an industry or firm, can still have a rather blinkered view on many issues. One important area, which might need external intervention, includes the emotional aspects, probably born of long established (internal) friendships, incidents etc. I do suspect that my presence (without sounding arrogant) could have indeed satisfied a strong ego trip for some of these people. Thinking back, I would guess that some of these characters might have been advisers themselves in their earlier lives.

It would be obvious to anyone that a prospect may well demonstrate a combination of more than one of the above categories. That would make it even more complicated for a consultant to nail down and to offer the ideal response. This chapter has demonstrated quite clearly that a consultant's life is, most of the time, a rather challenging one.

Chapter 5

Getting Information and Case Studies

Without accurate and appropriate client information, consultants will undoubtedly fail. In my experience, 99% of my clients have realised that it would be pointless if I were not furnished with the whole truth about them. Otherwise, the result could mean weak conclusions and ineffectual help and advice due to poor focus. They would have then wasted their investment, and wasted my time when I could have more usefully used it to help someone else instead. Their people might well be frustrated and felt demotivated too, as nothing would have been improved in their eyes. And, undoubtedly, this would be another reason for unfairly denigrating the consultants who had tried hard!

Questions to ask

Nevertheless, I have heard stories or indirect comments from consumers of consultancy that consultants are ineffective, disruptive, expensive, inexperienced etc. To be fair, some blame must lie with those guilty consultants themselves. As the first step, the latter ought to understand fairly well the intricate dynamics and culture of the businesses they have been contracted to assist. Identifying all the stakeholders of the project and understanding their wide variety of motivations is essential. In most cases, answers should be found (or rather, be unreservedly given) to the following questions asked of the interviewees and from the clients' perspectives: -

> What's the chief purpose(s) of this exercise?
> What's in it for me (the interviewee)?
> How will I, my friends/colleagues/bosses be affected – now and ultimately?
> Can I trust this person or interviewer with my frank revelations and possibly implicate myself as a direct result?

How much should I say?
Will I be informed of the outcomes of this exercise?
Will things be really better as a result?

Part of my strategy is to maximise empathy and not be wrong-footed at the beginning. This is critical for a mutually successful outcome and hopefully, a long-term business relationship. What are the best questions to ask, when and how to ask these, and who should provide the answers have to be decided. From my estimation, over 90% of my questions have been answered fairly honestly. It is always very few who are apprehensive about my presence, as indicated by the above questions. Probably they themselves have been tarred as the 'culprits' or wrongdoers in their organisations. Maintaining the status quo is definitely their natural preference. Again, good communication skills (e.g. positive body language) and a sincere approach can normally work wonders when dealing with these people.

Typical categories of clients in this context are: the Tell-all, Few-worders and Half-willing. There are others with combinations of these to varying degrees of relevance.

It can be quite a task to cut short a Tell-all's rambling speech, wordiness and enthusiasm. A good analogy is the water gushing from a malfunctioning fire hydrant. They have often caused me to overrun my time-bound interviews. In those situations, it could be rather difficult to stop their flow of information. Frequently, they would need to be reminded of the current question without my appearing curt. Nevertheless, some of their words are often gems of wisdom and full of insights, which can help illuminate the consultant's path of discovery. A paradoxical situation can also happen. Sometimes, prospects offload their worries onto consultants because the latter are the first to lend them a sympathetic and apparently free ear. However, these prospects sometimes forget that sensitive or strategic information could be used subsequently, not necessarily and always to their benefit. I often get the impression that these prospects themselves might feel somewhat triumphant too, afterwards, having had the rare opportunity to defend their own actions and viewpoints. This is because they have succeeded in not having to take on the consultant's offer of help!

The Few-worders tend to just answer my questions quite succinctly, appearing not to volunteer an extra word, let alone additional information, even though the latter might be relevant. It is like pulling hen's teeth! They were normally willing to contribute, but in their minds, somehow, they would seem to know exactly when to stop their contribution. Watching their body language would often offer the clues or explanation. It was likely that they were introverts by nature or might actually be holding some sort of grudge against someone, including their employer. However, I would normally prefer to attribute this behaviour to their personality and negative personal experiences of working in that firm. In critical situations, it would mean putting in the extra ounce of effort to coax out the other vital details, essential to complete my jigsaw. It would also be a personal challenge to encourage even further contributions. In a few cases, finding the cause(s) of their reticence might give useful and interesting clues to solving my client's problems.

Fortunately, the other category of the Half-willing often forms the minority. They are the ones who show varying degrees of apprehension in speaking to me, the outsider. Their main distinction from the Few-worders was their basic nature as extroverts. But something else might well prevent their full contributions. The one main impression I might get was one of fear, basically of what I might possibly ask and the consequences to themselves due to the answers they would give. It could indicate an obvious sign of serious organisational problems where openness was probably not encouraged. Perhaps a merger was rumoured (catalysed by recent poor corporate performance) with some expected redundancies. Internal politicking might be rife against a backdrop of backbiting and backstabbing. Probably, the bosses were autocrats and they ruled firmly using fear as their preferred technique. I have heard of cases where the interviewees had refused to tell the consultants anything.

Fortunately, I have never experienced that degree of refusal ...yet! In some cases, those interviewed were probably the guilty party (from their facial expressions and body language), i.e. causes of the problems in the first place. Thus, it would seem unlikely that the whole truth could be pried directly from their mouths! It might be the case of what is omitted is more important than what is uttered.

An external category of people is that of the direct customers of one's clients. This would normally apply when a survey was conducted on this extended contact base as part of the project. My experience has generally been quite positive with this group. They would normally reveal a great deal in response to my probing questions if they could be given certain reassurances about confidentiality. The setting or timing must be congenial too. Not all surveyed would demand confidentiality. A minority would very clearly say to me that their answers could be quoted verbatim. Obviously, the questions should be well thought out and phrased to suit the situation. With good experience, it was possible to detect the state of mind of the interviewee on the telephone. With a good indication of professionalism from us, the interview would always be useful. Again, common sense was needed in deciding the length of the conversation backed by a good, initial introduction. A few might try, rightly or wrongly to hold back giving their true answers or decide to pass this chore to another person, who would then become the 'victim' of my questions!

What can one see?

For the novice consultant, much can be gleaned by opening one's eyes all the time, without the need to even utter a word or listen. Having literally been to hundreds of companies, my descriptions of these and instant perceptions can easily fill up many paragraphs.

I have been to several shantytown look-alikes in my travels. The company name might have bits missing or appeared to be partly sun bleached out of existence. This was almost a sure sign of being financially deprived or just a sheer lack of image consciousness. Or, they might be too busy attacking internal fires to notice these negative signals, which were broadcast so obviously to the outside world. If image is an important factor for success, it is also a good starting point for me to ask.

The car park can often be an interesting place of discovery and learning too. If they have got one, what is its size? Are you expected to skilfully manoeuvre into the tightest of spots? Is it well kept or full of weeds, potholes and rubbish? Are the marked spaces generous or were they squeezed tightly to encourage the inevitable knocks/scrapes and time wasted in making several, very cautious vehicular manoeuvres? Do they really care enough to allocate 'visitor' and 'disabled' spaces or worry more about reserved lots (with specified initials, job titles and personalised numbers) for the big wigs only? One should also notice the makes and conditions of the cars in the car park. What do the bosses drive, as compared to the hoi polloi? Are there differentiations classes of gander and goose? Is it well kept or are there signs of overgrown weeds and scattered litter?

Out in the sticks off the M3 motorway, I was informed by one company that they were in surviving mode. I was therefore not surprised to discover that the managing director/owner drove an old Vectra banger. If one sees shiny 4x4s, Jags, Bentleys, Mercedes, it might pay to note their conditions, and also make note of any prevalence and vintage of their number plates.

Some companies have displays of nicely framed mission statements proudly embellishing their reception areas. But do look out for one with the word, 'Horizon', an ex-client company which I can proudly claim to have helped effect some positive change before its sale to a US buyer. Some receptionists would just smile wryly or shrug their shoulders when I queried them about these statements' significance. This is because many employees regard them as unnecessary. Having an impressive mission statement is equivalent to having a smart usherette in a theatre or a doorman: things have not been left to chance. If properly constitutcd, one can thereby be aware of the company vision, strategies, values and objectives.

The reception area is often the place where a visitor will have his first experience of the company. This can vary from just standing room space outside a homemade, grimy looking sliding glass 'kitchen' type window to a 1000 sq ft airy and expensive affair laid out with prime leather sofas and matching decor. There might be a grubby, torn and tatty vinyl floor or thick woolly Axminster type carpeting. There may even have a choice of free drinks on offer in the lush lounge area to sip while waiting. Is there a full time receptionist in attendance or a DIY, pick-phone-up affair? Are the receptionists smiling naturally or do they seem too flustered – the result of unreasonable multitasking and under manning? Is the corporate logo gleaming proudly in mint condition or just a cheap, tacky job, probably painted amateurishly many moons ago?

Watching the staff come and go into the reception area can also be fun and an eye opener. What are they dressed in? Are they in smart uniforms? Do they look happy or just seem to ignore you even if you could be a good potential customer? What are they doing or preoccupied with, and how are they interacting with their colleagues? Answers to these can provide good clues to their company culture. Ultimately, this can be useful in gauging their problems and interest in engaging you.

I have been to companies where the managing directors occupy a grubby room or 'pig sty', and occasionally be next to another manager (his right hand person?). In the premises of a Harrowian manufacturer, I sat on a chair that should have been dumped in the recycling skip many years ago. The floors were worn, filthy, full of holes and grimy, a reminder of Victorian or even Dickensian times. The office furniture was not any better; well worn by years of frictional contacts with many bottoms and possibly obtained fourth-hand from a car boot sale. Not surprising, to this day, I am still waiting for their decision to proceed on a 'high value' £12k marketing exercise. This contrasted sharply with a London SW1 based multi-storied, hi-tech building where I was standing on thickly piled lush carpets, next to crystal clear, thick tinted glass panes, overlooking a main road. In the meeting room, the 'designer' cutlery seemed to be in tiptop highly polished condition, and it was complemented with seats made of top quality expensive leather. Sadly, I have not been back since this 'mining' company has performed very well in the London FTSE and seemed to have been acquired.

It would appear pretty conclusive that companies which could not afford even a minimal level of investment on their physical, public image, are unlikely to afford consultants. This has been proven on countless occasions. Those with a mediocre standard of appearance might also be victims of cash flow problems or have failed to invest in the priority areas. Working for these companies might thus mean that getting your invoices paid would incur considerably more effort than usual.

Insights relating to types of projects and solutions

Executing the agreed proposals can be fraught with invisible manholes (i.e. pitfalls) and potential dangers. There have been cases of clients misunderstanding my proposals and intentions. Hidden agendas at board level can be particularly tricky and hazardous to one's consulting career path. Lack of explanations or clear communications prior to my appearance might mean that I must explain my presence to every Donna, Derek and Ali. This situation is unhelpful to everyone concerned since there can be serious instances where people's jobs are on the line, including the managing director's.

Over the years, I have taken on the challenge of tackling a wide variety subjects. Invariably, they fall under the three broad categories of HR/performance, operations/manufacturing and sales/marketing. What follows is really a synopsis of the key issues and solutions I have recommended.

I helped an engineering company to survive by researching potential customers for him. It was a challenge as I had to use my network of contacts and some insider knowledge. In this instance, there were no holds barred. He was definitely a Tell-all. Only about three years ago, this company was doing just OK under the current managing director's father. The latter founded the company but it had gradually lost focus and a sense of reality by investing unwisely in machines at high capital cost without much prospect of a reasonable return. Clearly, they were victims of the keeping up with the Joneses syndrome, aiming to be at the leading edge of technology and hoping to impress their customers.

An interesting area, which has perennial interest and evokes some degree of emotion, concerns staff motivation and morale. Several of my clients suffered from this particular weakness. It is also a surprisingly hard area in which to quantify accurately their particular degree of seriousness. A highly task-orientated culture would naturally put concern-for-people issues lower down the list of corporate focus. The focus would normally be on financial performance, appropriate returns and success. However, it is always a great mistake to be unbalanced in that way with this bias. One client in the IT sector was oblivious to a similar situation with their techies.

Another client in the logistics field suffered very low morale and was even given negative scores according to a few staff members. There was visible stress and the common symptom of staff turnover was present. My approach was to impart my knowledge of relieving stress, improving their structural hierarchies, and effect an overhaul of their recruitment processes. As an organisation focusing on operations and sales turnover, they had forgotten that their fast growth could impose strains on their structures. Top management had to know too and be made aware of how people would respond to different types of motivations and rewards. Top management also needed to bear their responsibility for certain types of 'demotivating' behavioural patterns, which normally emanated from themselves.

This client was also unconsciously, a victim of the notorious vicious circle of serious symptoms. These were low morale, high staff turnover, inequitable salary structure, weak management, excessive workload (capacity issue) and customer pressures. My key challenge was to convince senior management of the serious predicament they were in then. Immediate, remedial actions were required. As an 'operations' based company, whose unique selling point (USP) was in processing international cargo movements, any excessive haemorrhage of experienced staff (especially to an aggressive local competitor) must be viewed as potentially disastrous. One affected area was the immediate drop in customer service and delivery. My key role was to offer a fast track coaching programme of the management team, from the ops directors down. I also felt the need to guide them in applying some of the recommendations set out in my succinct report.

Much has been written on conflict resolution. The optimist would rightly say that 'healthy' conflicts can be potentially beneficial. But there is a fine line between the healthy and destructive categories. Common sense says that those who have climbed to the upper echelons of management might bear certain personality traits. Competitiveness, authoritarianism, task orientation, high achievement and power needs, visible assertiveness and 'non-team' working are regarded as common examples of the latter. Each director might well have his idea of strategic direction for the company. Hence it is not surprising that conflicts normally exist, especially at the top levels.

Not long afterwards, I was asked to assist this client's sister company based in Scotland. This company had enjoyed phenomenal growth for many years but as usual, times had changed. History had somehow repeated itself in terms of the above well-known vicious circle. The recent managing director too, had apparently 'failed' for reasons of poor preparation and 'unfavourable' situational circumstances. Any top dog should be made aware of the relative 'toughness' and the inevitable politics that had often reared its head. Thus my conclusions emphasised the need for an urgent replacement of the managing director, who must assume early control of the rapidly deteriorating situation. Without a clearly strong and visible captain at the rudder, its ship would inevitably be heading for the rocks. After that, my role was focused on rebuilding the new team, ensuring a successful transition of its new managing director. Issues concerning conflicting personalities, emotional intelligence (EI), attitudes, leadership styles, delegation, performance management, teambuilding and motivation also required attention.

Another subset of clients involves conflicts within family businesses. Typically, the founder will clearly want to ensure continual success in the present and future, into perpetuity. As evident in most living creatures, a tough, pioneering approach almost always guarantees survival in the early stages of their life cycles. However, once established and after some time later, this attitude and its attendant philosophies may assume less significance and appropriateness in the next phase of 'growth' and stability. Also, the days of 'command and follow' may be over. The young 'Turks/Tartars', who are conditioned in the modern techniques might well have different ideas and thoughts. The latter may have an easier life by milking the business, as the issue of survival has probably become a distant memory. Hence, you then have the ready mixed ingredients for potentially serious conflicts between the various generations.

An interesting case involved the founding boss who had regular rows with his female financial controller. It was a small company and their rows would literally reverberate throughout the whole firm when they occurred. During my investigation, the financial controller did recognise and admitted her erroneous behaviour, partly attributing that to her combative type personality. Interestingly, what also transpired was that she had grown rather envious of her female colleague, a service manageress, who was apparently given preferential treatment by the boss. She, allegedly, also had had an affair with the boss!

Sometimes, I have come across 'rough diamonds' amongst the managers. Typically, they were promoted by virtue of their superior job performance in a specialist job function, and not for their proven management prowess. To make matters worse, companies would make do rather than invest in focused, corrective mentoring (akin to some positive awakening) for these people. The end results could be poor management, weak corporate/functional performance, ineffective leadership and low morale. However, not all personalities take kindly to being mentored or be asked to embrace behavioural change. This can be the case if those who are targeted to be mentored have been particularly successful.

So what could possibly be done in cases of serious internal conflict?

First, it always pays to obtain an objective evaluation of their seriousness and an accurate assessment of the sources and root causes (if possible). Invariably, my approach involves helping all the relevant parties to fully understand and realise their contributions, and also the resulting consequences to themselves and company. I might also act as an impartial mediator, which can be an interesting and challenging role to undertake when a high level of trust is essential, backed by good understanding. Also, one must be interested in assuming such a role, and it is vital to be exceptionally alert to the unexpected in such interventions. Normally, both parties are encouraged to problem solve and collaborate. Ultimately, the aim must be to remove the main root causes to these conflicts and help re-establish fresh environments where future conflicts can be recognised and effectively tackled. Helping them to refocus their energies to become higher-level performers and be more competitive is always welcome. Team building is often cited as a solution to reduce harmful conflicts. There is often no smoke without fire. People can rightly feel aggrieved if they have been unfairly treated and have not been given their due recognition.

An important subject is people performance. Most prospects and clients say, 'There is always room for improvement', which is broadly true. The key question is, 'What does one want to improve and to what extent of change would one be satisfied with?'

From exposure to many companies, poor performance can be attributed to many possible causes. Ignorance on the part of the poor performer about his personal performance is common. This is because superiors might have conveniently turned a blind eye to such situations, which were deemed not serious in the past. Having highlighted poor performance, the pressure then exists to remedy the situation now to prevent its recurrence and further deterioration. A standard solution is via a performance appraisal. Setting up and successfully establishing effective performance appraisals can be tough, even for the true professionals. In reality, not many companies can run these well. Organisations that are satisfied with their appraisals have invariably benefited from good pragmatic design, invested in training all round, and fine tuned over a time period, aiming to improve further. There will always be a minority of companies that ignore the benefits of a good appraisal system.

Recruiting the best person for the identified job is always a good long-term strategy and solution. Recruitment can be an excellent opportunity to vet the candidate for his attitudes, intelligence, personality traits, skills, experience etc. For example, are the attitudes congruent with the employer's culture and values? If not, is it reasonable then to expect the company to adapt totally to this new blood, instead of the other way round? What can one do about ingrained, incompatible attitudes? Much attention must be given to the interviewer's competence and the possible use of appropriate exercises and psychometric tests to highlight potential problems. Many examples of such tests exist but they need to be picked for their specific relevance, proven reliability and validity. Some tests have proved to be more popular and are used more widely due to very aggressive marketing and focused product development on certain features. Ultimately, it is a case of 'horses for courses'. Ignorance can also be bliss as there are countless tests on the market. It is not surprising that, as a result of some previous bad experience, there exist many sceptics in regard to such tests.

'Herzberg's hygiene factors' should be remembered for their relevance to both motivation and job performance. I have seen situations when people were cramped into tight spaces, drinks had to be paid for and taking of one's holidays was unreasonably restricted. There could be an excessive number of unreasonable rules imposed by autocratic management. This could often stifle the much needed empowerment where people could use their own initiatives.

Fundamental issues such as working without good job descriptions and clearly defined job roles are relatively common. Although some degree of flexibility is always welcome and to be built in, some people may prefer a more structured set-up as far as their tasks are concerned. This is particularly true for some employees who do not have much freedom and authority within their job positions. Similarly, other individuals require closer supervision or direction and should be given more (expected) regular feedback. As organisations evolve under multifaceted demands, some roles need to be redefined periodically to reflect the existing realities.

Closely related to performance is the area of leadership, another well-publicised area where much has been written and published. The consensus seems that building strong, cohesive teams after having selected the right team members should be a high priority. The subject of emotional intelligence can be particularly relevant when poor morale rears its big ugly head. Put simply, the idea of emotional intelligence focuses on the softer side of humans, ensuring that good leadership incorporates the subtleties of good people management. I believe that top management should be of the highest overall quality and requires wise, strategic decision-making. Other useful attributes would be having good ideas (and being open to new ones), a tough outlook (not being too ruthless) and practising good time management. A strong desire to be popular, unwillingness to accept any blame and a strong desire to be liked would be definitely negatives. One such managing director did fall out of favour by not accepting any blame, and by being unwilling to modify even slightly his behaviour.

My usual solution for clients to improve performance is highly targeted, executive, one-to-one coaching or mentoring. As I have a very strong interest in human behaviour and motivation, this has been my main preoccupation and activity for more than 20 years. It is common to observe that senior managers find themselves where they are now, running the show, probably by default or their own design. Those who have been through my hands have been keen to learn key management and leadership skills quickly in order to save their own skins and possibly to avoid or reduce embarrassing failures! At the same time, they have also received invaluable ongoing perceived feedback on their actual performance. The latter could be unpalatable or psychologically painful to accept if it was dished out *carte blanche* with 100% negatives and not tempered with a modicum of good, positive asides.

A fairly common dilemma involved weak leadership in companies offering professional services. One client had struggled for four years before they were persuaded to tackle their unsatisfactory pain level. They had the urge to do something about the situation but were torn by internal disputes (amongst the directors) and poor focus of priorities. Good strategies in marketing their services effectively and visible leadership were sadly lacking. Their managing director and chairman were also naturally fairly weak, unassertive personality types. But how could you best persuade people to modify their innate personalities? Having good specialist knowledge internally, over several niches of their industry was their saviour. Other issues were relatively early disillusionment of their graduate employees, low-margin projects and the stifling of their middle managers by internal processes. After coaching the latter and a number of board level workshops, they were well on their way to moving forward more confidently and were projecting a fairly united front.

As a qualified NLP (neuro linguistics programming) practitioner, I can normally delve deep enough into my clients' minds to perform some short, sharp 'magical' techniques to help boost their confidence levels. Thus, my achievements to date include tackling the fear of flying, fear of cold calling, boosting low self-esteem and helping clients to acquire the self-confidence to confront awkward situations.

On top of most companies' agenda will be sales and more sales, ideally profitable ones.

At least 35% of my projects have had some sales element to them. That is to be expected since we all know that without customers, there is no business. So, what are the main issues that I have encountered in this challenging area?

If sales rely on personal selling, it must be down to the calibre of the sales people. What criteria were used to select them in the first place? There were frequent cases of square pegs in oval holes – a semi-satisfactory state of affairs and a real obstacle. Are the rewards appropriate to the level of sales and specific industry to ensure a fundamental, high level of motivation? A high basic payment without commission can spell disaster for certain categories of selling. One based merely on commission can prove attractive and motivating if the sky is the real limit. How good is their manager or director at providing the right kind of leadership, motivation and ongoing monitoring support? The top salesman may not necessarily be able or keen to indulge in keeping others in line, that is, playing the manager's role. Internal processes and systems can be important in giving the ongoing infrastructure and support. The tendering process, image, competitive pricing, PR, effective strategies/tactics are the other main aspects to consider. Occasionally, the customer-facing skills can be improved upon by focusing on situational body signals and paying good attention to interactions with prospects and customers. All the above mentioned normally only cover the main internal issues and perspectives.

One case concerned a designer and manufacturer of lift components. It was a small family business that had been fairly successful competing against the 'bigger' boys, so to speak. However, as resources were limited, their sales and marketing strategies lacked good focus and direction. Price competitiveness was expected to be a key factor but it turned out not to be critical. My involvement helped them to better exploit their limited investments in exhibitions, marketing materials and website. Their sales resources were redirected to cover the critical elements of the sales process. Again, an external catalyst can act as coordinator/overseer and monitor of cost effective actions.

Another client in the packaging industry had survived but had ambitious aims to increase their sales significantly. Through objective investigation and partly due to historical reasons, their internal sales competences were regarded as sadly below average. Reorganising internal roles and that of their product managers would help to increase their currently below average conversion ratios. Boosting their sales management effectiveness and a review of other marketing elements (pricing, exhibitions, products portfolio, selling skills) did make some appreciable differences.

To ensure complete coverage, one should also consider all the external, relevant, objective perspectives of my clients' customers. This was only possible if the customers' honest opinions were elicited. On most occasions, the resulting efforts made to survey the customers were worthwhile. Some interesting comments that my clients' customers made were 'arrogant, inefficient, late in delivering, unresponsive to requests, expensive, and technically incompetent'.

The fact that a company was regarded as 'arrogant' meant that their customers had been forced at that time, probably having no choice but to buy from them. Inevitably, other competitors would grab this advantage of this precarious state to gain favour and enter the fray to compete. The remedy was some form of internal cultural change, probably, aiming to be more customer aware, be more focused and responsive.

As a Chartered Engineer (mechanical and production) by profession, I have tackled several production related challenges for my clients. The main subjects revolved around boosting of high quality production output, achieving zero defects, maximising process efficiencies (supply chain) and reducing lead times. There would be times when I would help clients to identify 'waste' (*muda* in Japanese) within their systems. Idle times, over production, over stocking, sub-optimal layouts causing unnecessary movements are the main examples of traditional 'waste' that should be eliminated. Traditional tools such as cell manufacturing, TQM (total quality management), six sigma, BPR (business process reengineering), JIT (just in time, as opposed to JIC – just in case), 5S can often be used successfully. Knowing the techniques is only half the battle. Much depends on knowing which technique to use, and where, how and when to apply it. Common sense dictates that the most progressive organisations are familiar with how to apply all these proven techniques. If not, one would question the reasons for such ignorance.

The other area of success involves cultural change. Many factors can come in here and these have to be considered. North American and traditional British cultures differ significantly but one could definitely learn a few things from the other. Americans tend to be very results-focused and be direct and clear-cut in their approach, not mincing too many words. The British tend to prefer not to rock the boat, placing high importance in friendships, old business relationships, some consensual activities and above other things, in retaining some tradition. Also, a longer-term perspective with added caution is more common amongst British companies.

Amongst my successes was the case of a typically traditional British automotive manufacturer, which had been run using an autocratic management style for years. Thus, empowerment was non-existent and the top man vetted most decisions. Use of initiative was limited. The managing director was apparently ready to change for the better, but the key question was really 'How to do so?' The company had sustained steady growth and numbered 180 strong when I arrived. By the end of my assignment, they had grown to over 240. Their technology lay in sensible but traditional designs of simple mechanical components. Their process type layouts had incurred waste of various types. They were introduced to the Manufacturing Cells concept. Essentially, I ran several problem-solving workshops, imparting key knowledge on mundane but essential tools in communications, meetings etc. I saw it as my role to encourage and offer them good ideas on how decisions could be made within a supportive team culture. My few months there, spent chairing some of their meetings, resulted in a real cultural change whereby problem-solving teams were educated and encouraged to use individual initiative. Several issues concerning lead times, quality and delivery were tackled successfully. This resulted in great and effective communication throughout, enhanced self-reliance and a highly responsive organisational structure. Managers had made progress and a few were promoted. Various philosophies of TQM, zero defects and World Class philosophies were also adopted. Quite soon after, the company was sold to a US conglomerate for a 'good' price. The main reward for my efforts came from the last feedback I received, that people were now happy, getting on with their problem solving and had 'no further need' of my services!

Another case involved an IT company where every functional head had their own ideas and was at loggerheads with the CEO. There was much infighting, disagreements and a blatant lack of direction. On top of all that, the quality of management was considered to be poor. So far, I have managed to reduce conflicts through behavioural change and shared established norms of leadership, and I have given them reassurance and good ideas about how to move forward. With the addition of better-qualified and appropriate staff members, they can now look ahead to more stability.

Finally, an interesting project involved a market leader in an engineering/production firm, who was a market leader in producing a synthetic material. Strategic design and direction was weak and there was a noticeable imbalance of power at board level. The chief executive had his hands partly tied by a working 'investor', who had a very strong, dominating personality. Their key symptoms included a 'cannot do attitude', and they were production-focused to the detriment of customer orientation. It was a case of 'buy what we make' and not necessarily, 'what would you want, Mr Customer'? This was confirmed in our survey of their customers, which highlighted an 'arrogant' attitude mentioned by a high percentage of their own customers. Sales and marketing had been weak due to a flawed structure. Resource allocations and focus by the chief of sales were ineffective. This function was reorganised, strengthened with new 'sales blood'. The latter was recruited for their more pro-active approach and better fitting sales personality profiles. My challenge was to expose this strong power domination within operations, which had restricted the benefits of earlier initiatives. I used a customised 360 degrees tool with individual feedback to highlight the prevailing attitudes. The result was a company which had become more sensitised to the symptoms with noticeable modifications to the managers' attitudes. Steps were taken to be more attentive to customers' needs. To be expected, the strong personality apparently wanted to retain overall control on any future training/development issues. They were given recommendations on reducing the deleterious effects and on how to develop a stronger, healthier culture.

Chapter 6   Tips for Clients and Prospects

This is especially written with clients or potential clients in mind. This is because prospects are often secretly curious about consulting in general and clients might also welcome some 'less direct' feedback.

I have hardly pulled any punches with anyone, especially with clients. However, my life in general could have been more exciting, fulfilling or usefully lived if clients had been made aware of their own shortcomings. This could have encouraged them to act more appropriately and responsibly for everyone's benefits. There is some truth in the trite 'customers are always right'. To me in practice, it translates to agreeing as much as possible with the customers so that they are kept reasonably happy and will continue to pay our wage bills. From an integrity viewpoint, what they themselves want might not be the same as what they truly desperately need! This interesting dichotomy can have a significant impact on a consultant's income.

Some of my comments here may have been touched on elsewhere. In fact, this may be regarded as a summary with good relevance for clients, who may rightly claim the lack of time to read my whole book. This very short chapter itself may make rewarding reading on its own. For this reason alone, I have kept my lips succinct and complete.

My main tips for you, the clients, especially prospects, are:

'Time is money' – a cliché subscribed to by most serious professionals. Let us maximise the use of such a rare commodity by being honest and open, with the minimum amount of 'game playing'. Do say what you think and say what you really do want to say, i.e. best cut to the chase.
There is a suspicion that the traditional British tendency is not to utter the brutal truth. Another critical aspect involves the big consumer of time, i.e. agreeing to meet and subsequently

cancelling or postponing the meeting umpteen times. Indeed, there is much time wasted through coaching or workshop sessions being postponed. Such wasted time could often be more productively used. Another real bugbear would be about your non-appearance at the appointed place and time.

Playing politics amongst yourselves is fine (but note that it is probably to your own ultimate detriment and financial loss). However, we consultants need to earn a living and involving us in your political games will not give us much satisfaction, just mere frustration. We would need to disentangle the politicking, thus enabling us to get to the heart(s) of your matter quickly. The main consequence of politicking could probably mean a bigger bill for you to settle. You may also end up by not being 100% happy with the final results or our diagnosis.

Please refrain from offering us false hope of winning any work from you. If you do not have the slightest intention of investing a fair and reasonable sum for your own betterment, please refrain from requesting for costly proposals. In a competitive market, such as consulting, we can accept your prerogative of shopping around but we would be grateful to know about that intention too. For example, you may wish to compare our offering against your current favourite consultant; a common practice which we do acknowledge. It is likely that consultants' proposals are not ideally designed for the DIY market. If you were capable of resolving your own problems internally, it is very likely that you would not be predisposed to seek external assistance. However, it is a very common human streak to seek something for free. Unfortunately for yourself, you may well end up 'paying' something, even indirectly and without you being fully conscious or aware of it.

Think carefully before agreeing to our proposals, which are invariably and specifically designed to help you or solve your pressing problems. As commercial 'animals' ourselves, we would expect some degree of hard negotiating. However, once we have shaken on the deal, chickening out by either side is not really acceptable or ethical. Those of you who lack total integrity and delight in this practice have probably been highlighted in this book.

Try to be clear, realistic and be pragmatic, as regards what you would really want us to achieve for you. If this is impossible to fulfil, why not be totally honest enough to say so, ideally at the beginning? As experts (most of us should be) on human psychology, we will understand and should be happy and, normally we will be able to help you. A high degree of frankness can be extremely helpful to everyone concerned. Expecting miracles from fellow mortals (including consultants!) is unrealistic. But, you have the right to expect or even demand objectivity, insights and plentiful of useful ideas.

Only a handful of my clients have asked me for references, whom they would want to contact directly. This may be seen as normal business practice in selecting a service supplier. However, it is a fact that very few people would normally offer negative comments in case of undesirable repercussions. Selection should be based on various 'competence' related criteria and the presence of good chemistry or compatibility between you and your would-be consultant. In some cases, I have refused point blank to offer any of my clients' names if I sense the situation as negative, i.e. facing a Timewaster (see Chapter 4). In such instances, this prospect might have other ulterior motives in his mind.

A 'better' way to check out a consultant's ability would be to give a simple test using various scenarios. It would then be the case of 'taste before you buy'. Any consultant worth his salt and by his experience, should be able to arm himself with the ideal responses to most hypothetical situations. The prospect must avoid being an irritating Brainpicker! Since you are paying, you will have the right to pick your choice. Hopefully, it is the 'best' choice available to suit your needs.

Once you have contracted us to help in an initiative, subsequent contracting out psychologically and dumping the whole mess onto us would be somewhat non beneficial and unproductive, for you. We are normally at our best working in partnership with you to effect the improvements that you have sought in the first place. We are also best at delivering our promises against what we have mutually agreed. Do open fully your hearts and let us know; we are definitely not good mind readers!

Finally, consultants can only react as normal humans. We have chosen to advise etc. As sincere professionals, we can often offer you a true lifeline for your business.

Chapter 7   Yes! Tips for Consultants

Since no consulting book is complete without a few words of guidance for its fellow consultants, I have ventured to leave some in this chapter. What I have postulated here has mainly come from my years of observations and interactions. These are predominantly my personal views and conclusions. Obviously, clients and prospects are allowed into this chapter and they may well find something informative if not interesting. At least they will now understand that proper consulting is definitely not as easy as it appears to be. People who have spent much of their time in corporate life have subsequently returned to it after brief 'unrewarding' spells as consultants. Dipping their toes into consulting waters might not be to their liking. From my own mistakes, I have also tried to portray what it is really like from the consultant's perspective.

There must be many thousands of so-called consultants, advisers, mentors, coaches and such like. One key question is: 'Why should someone buy from one and not from another'? If you examine yourself critically, you may not like what you see, thereby coming to a discouraging conclusion. Do you have the necessary experience and expertise, which you can confidently offer? Even if you have the essential know-how, can you perform remarkably well enough to consistently offer a high level of client satisfaction?

Key personality traits

First, it is the issue of having the right combination of relevant personality traits. As I have alluded to before, intelligent persistence is certainly essential to ensure success in obtaining work. This must be the true test of success. I have come across many fellow consultants who have lacked the mental stamina and emotional resilience to succeed. In reality, this means persisting till the practical end with a targeted prospect even though the immediate prospect of any work forthcoming might appear almost zero. People do change their minds; it is a matter of timing and being convinced. Indeed, it is a trait which has been used and aimed at myself by a few of my 'hunters'! I do have real life examples where someone else in my shoes could have easily given up on a prospect but I have persisted. Sometimes, I have been rewarded eventually, after investing several years' efforts. As time goes on, you can become wiser as to when you should give up the chase and call it a day.

As explained, persistence is essential but you have to be realistic too and be slightly sensitive to the circumstances. It might be the case of 'throwing in the towel' after a certain point. There have been many occasions when I have felt that, if the truth be known, I have invested enough time, energy and pennies in my efforts to convince certain prospects of my worth. There are reasons, whether justified or not, for not eliciting a positive response. Some reasons have been mentioned earlier on. I think that some of the main ones are:

- Resistance, reluctance or inability to accept outside help
- Your competitors have already established a strong psychological foothold
- There is no strong perceived need for any help and/or desire/ability to pay for it
- Your expertise etc. are not what is apparently sought
- There may be something 'unacceptable' about you or your company.

Hence persistence should be moderated with a modicum of intelligent awareness.

Being immersed in others' problems and tempered with a strong desire to help can make it difficult to withdraw yourself psychologically and physically from the situation. You might well conclude that the opportunity cost attributed to some of the 'wasted' time could well be regarded as high. Hence, would it be more productive to pursue other alternatives instead? There might be fresher or tastier fish in the pond. How good are you in reading the situation accurately enough to be right? Are there obvious signs of disinterest, bordering on passive rejection?

One relevant instance concerned a good-sized packaging company (design and manufacture) where I spent much time, both onsite with three successive managing directors and offsite (thinking) over an elapsed period of two years. Eventually, I just had to cut myself off from this business relationship, cutting my losses, as my partner would say. I will now attempt to justify my action. The managing directors and their subordinates I interviewed would just use my sessions to inform me of their past and current actions, interspersed with spatters of currently perceived weaknesses. I was expected to listen and respond to those situations. My attempts to offer structured help would be met with various plausible replies and the need for further meetings with other people. In retrospect, I concluded that these managing directors would not make a decision (in my favour) to proceed since they would always able to find subtle objections due to the complexities involved. For example, consultants had been involved in the past and I was expected to help identify and even to rectify the 'leftovers' during those meetings without any hint of payment! As consultants, we should take a clear lead in the how but even this initiative was somehow usurped by these managing directors. Also, some of the ideas that had discussed previously were subsequently implemented by someone internal.

Having a related trait termed 'thick-skinned' can often help persistence. In most sales type roles, it is inevitable that there will be a moderate to high level of rejections. The actual amount depends on luck and the use of intelligence. As my ex sales and marketing lecturer from the London Business School used to say, 'ultimately, it is a matter of how much serial rejection you can stomach without giving up'. That certainly contains much truth and can help to account for the high turnover of the 'weaker' sales people employed at the sharp end. Facing repeated rejections can be quite hard for most humans to accept. Not very many could survive (sometimes) the number of rejections to one's approaches that can occur relentlessly, day in and day out. Naturally, these include the thousands of self-employed consultants who have to hunt for work to survive. Hunting is a perennial, ongoing activity, necessary to refill the cash pot. Without a reasonable volume of sales, there will be nothing to sustain any business – this applies to consultants too.

I can remember quite clearly in my early days and months how demotivating and frustrating it could be, when even 50 phone calls did not result in an appointment. An appointment is normally the first step towards acquiring a project. We are not selling clearly defined commodities such as envelopes, paper clips or laser paper when orders can be expected over the phone. Selling consultancy is very different as it relies heavily on direct, personal face-to-face contact to convince the purchaser. It was also a case of being a victim of increasing self-doubts as to your ability to succeed, even at this first phase. As I have attempted to explain and illustrate in the earlier chapters, there can be infinite reasons as to why some people are not interested and probably won't buy at that particular time; and sometimes never. Nowadays, I have built up enough psychological *oomph* (equivalent to a psychological rubber aura) to withstand the disappointments and have refined my techniques to maximise my hit rates. One needs to determine a balance of the required efforts required versus the potential rewards. This leads conveniently to my next tip.

Another way of looking at persistence is to consider your self-confidence, a key supportive trait for success, especially in selling. This means having the innate strength to portray positively, outwardly your true capability and personality. Without self-confidence, it is unlikely that you can succeed as a consultant. Having this confidence is also a must for all those selling activities. Who in his right mind would contemplate buying from a supplier reeking of doubts about his own products or services? The danger can arise when you may feel overconfident and then slide dangerously into arrogance. It is true to observe that many a good consultant has apparently failed due to his inability to sell convincingly his wares.

Most good sales training professionals will advise putting in sufficient efforts into one key activity, which is essential to successful selling. This activity has to be preparation. Initially, this applies to your mental state, which must be at a high level of alertness to anticipate the reaction you get in response to your approach. There have been times when I have been stunned and left, feeling both embarrassed and frustrated at my state of mental unpreparedness to react properly in those sales situations. These outcomes could be the result of having previously been engaged in intensive mental activities or plainly speaking, just not been fully awake enough from a previous late night! There may even be certain times of the day or days of each month when you may not be at your intellectual peak. This is something worth determining. Good efforts should be invested in researching into your prospects and preparing for second-guessing about possible outcomes.

Timing

Even if your preparation is immaculate, there is this element of lady luck or perhaps one might say 'external timing' involved in some occasions. Events are happening all the time within most evolving organisations. This means that there are times when the prospects can be less receptive to external approaches to help them. Such times might be related to change(s) in management, other restructuring, initiatives where high level decisions have already been made to try various in-house ideas. The prospects themselves might even be under severe pressure to perform or deliver, without the option of using external help. Again, being alert enough to seek clarification can be very beneficial indeed. Another aspect of timing is mentioned below.

A good example relates to an IT client. The CEO had been fobbing me off for years till I managed to say the correct combination of persuasive words to him one day. If you have had several meetings and teleconferences, it is entirely feasible to construct a behavioural profile of your target. It is usually a case of advancing stealthily till there is no objection or reason left for not using my services. The fact that I have probably outlived many competitors' efforts must be compelling evidence enough or reason for this client to try me.

The issue of timing will apply to your prospects too. Knowing how and when they work, and the cycles they might be subject to, can be crucial to getting to meet them, and thus to winning the work. This is the time when you should attempt to befriend and charm the receptionist and PAs (traditionally gatekeepers, can sometimes be quite helpful!) if at all possible. These categories of insiders can be invaluable in guiding you through their complex internal maze of possibilities, even suggesting possible shortcuts. Occasionally, they can also lead you to your..... There have been times when their candour has tempered my dogged persistence! There was this well-established German firm that sell consumer products which I was allocated to make contact. The PA there hinted strongly that it would be a waste of my time trying to interest her German managing director. Thanks to her helpfulness, she gave me alternative contact names to pursue.

Other useful traits and targets

Simply put, consulting is about solving clients' problems. To do that, you need the required depth of knowledge and skills, which, ideally, make you stand out from the crowd. Consulting is definitely a crowded profession where supply apparently exceeds demand. Knowledge can certainly be acquired from the infinite sources, i.e. the internet, friends, books, courses, other literature, fellow consultants and professional networks. A more difficult aspect concerns your innate problem-solving skills and aptitudes. Certainly a strong interest in helping others is highly desirable. Enthusiasm is critically important as it can excite and be used to sway your target's mindset.

In my opinion, apart from the key personality traits already mentioned, other essential personal attributes/skills for a successful consultant are:

> Wisdom and gravitas to guide and lead
> Strong analytically
> Intelligent research and synthesising ability
> Application of cold, incisive logic (common sense?) to business/management issues
> Objective and impartial in approach
> Effective influencing and communication skills
> Good overview (unblinkered) of the bigger picture
> Survive amidst any dirty internal politics
> Has had exposure to many situations, thus leading to the 'seen it, done it' confidence

The above list raises a tough dilemma for many would-be consultants as regards the choice and how to begin. I can hear many say, 'One has to start somewhere.' That is true, but will that choice offer your potential client the little extra that they might be looking for in you? What is your track record? If you do not have one, how can you build one credibly? More importantly, can you sell enough business to earn a decent living? Like other professional services, we can be unwilling victims of the 'feast or famine' syndrome. It is certainly not encouraging and it is no fun sitting around with zilch income for weeks or months on end! Many projects have incubation periods of months, if they ever materialise at all.

Having made a start, should you offer expertise in one or more areas? Irrespective of your decision, there would naturally appear, subsequently, the need to maintain your freshness and uniqueness. This is not easy to accomplish as the numbers and range of competitors increase and evolve as you yourself would.

The trend has led some consultants to become a so-called niche player. What should one specialise in that can practically maintain your leading edge in the latest know-how? Know-how can be easily copied or repackaged into another fad. After all these years, I have concluded that 'to be all things to all men' would equal a lack of focus – a highly unattractive proposition for many clients, who would normally prefer to employ specialists. There is of course, room for the generalist, who can assist with most, if not all the so-called key issues. There is room for the generalist if that is the client's expectation and is considered a necessity for success with his problem. Specialists are, by definition can be very narrowly focused and hence are incapable of seeing the whole picture.

Hence, where you should draw the line would depend on the client's needs and perception and on how the consultant would like to pitch himself, thereby picking out the ideal segment. However, to succeed in consulting has never been a soft or easy option. It is about continually adapting and learning from mistakes, honing your skills and interests over a time period of enforced evolvement. Today's hot cakes (e.g. 6 Sigma, Lean) can soon become a stale, trite fad; desperately needing rebranding. The other pitfall is occupying too narrow a niche, which means that the task of locating the interested prospects can become extremely unproductive and tedious. Effectively, this would tantamount to locating a coin in a landfill!

In practice, it is advisable to have at hand all the essential information relating to the prospect and your corresponding 'best' arsenal of responses. The latter will invariably include answers to the objections normally encountered, your target's personal details and idiosyncrasies. As in most sales situations, objections should be regarded as positive indications of possible interest. Overcoming these successfully can sometimes lead to a positive outcome.

As part of your mental preparation, it is important that you pick the 'right' targets to approach in the first place. You should ask yourself why you have picked certain targets. Was it the industry segment, geographic area, culture, products, or other relevant factor that might have influenced your choices? For example, was there strong personal interest or do you have a special reason(s)? Your honest answers will give you the psychological support and essential self-motivation which can support your essential qualities of persistence and self confidence. For example, if you are one of those 'green' converts, who believe in conservation etc., you may be approaching someone in the chemical business with some degree of reluctance. If that is the case, you will have started off without a fully committed subconscious, genuinely tuned towards helping your target. Similarly, if you happen to despise or not respect a particular culture, organisation or individual, it would seem very sensible not to include them as your targets. It is unfortunate if your boss has allocated any of these personal 'undesirables' to you to contact. There had been occasions when I have not maintained subsequent contact with some individuals for the above reasons, after my initial contacts with them. Not only was there no rapport or detectable interest from the prospect, mutual respect might have seemed rather scarce. The well-known phrase 'familiarity breeds contempt' does apply well in consulting!

To succeed as an entrepreneur (independent consultants included), you should ideally possess a number of useful traits. You have to be opportunistic and be forever on the lookout for profitable deals, deals and more deals. How opportunistic are you or are you a routine-driven or passive type person? Another relates to risk taking; how much should you speculate, hoping to accumulate? I admit that on a number of occasions, I have made some promises to my clients, banking heavily on my intellect and strong ability to seek out excellent solutions, thus saving my skin. So far, I have managed, most of the time, to obtain the correct balance between my delivery of first class results and aiming to 'exceed my clients' expectations'. As I have often told my prospects, no two management/business problems are exactly the same. Hence, it is rather unlikely that the ideal solutions can just be conveniently lifted from the many shelves in my office. It would help if you have a highly motivating vision for yourself. This vision could just simply be achieving enough success to be comfortably off and having a list of 100% satisfied clients.

Support and partnerships

Like most self-employed entrepreneurs and businesses, it could make a big difference if you have good family support. This normally means strong psychological support and backing from your spouse/partner. A consultant's lifestyle is often a time consuming one and can incur extended time periods on site with clients. Spouses have told me that, apart from the long hours or periods away from home, they do enjoy the financial/material benefits. It would be better still if a family member can also periodically act as your devil's advocate when the need arises. As we know, (y) heads are normally better than (x), where $(x) < (y)$. Personally, I have been rather fortunate in this respect, thus far. However, heavy reliance on your spouse to bale you out is fantasy thinking.

Support can extend beyond your immediate family or social circles. Networking comes to mind here and I do invest a reasonable amount of my time and energies here. The logic is obvious; someone you know may lead you to someone else, who may present you with a business opportunity. The key word here is 'opportunity', not a contract (agreed piece of paid work). You still need to pursue such opportunities and be hopeful of clinching a deal of reasonable monetary value. Sometimes, fellow networkers can offer tips and guidance, which may provide clarity and reassurance to your own situations. In my case, my virtual network of contacts runs into thousands. This is due to my professional memberships with several bodies and institutions. However, I must say that total reliance on networking for financial returns would have been disastrous, in my case. My personal philosophy is to be self-reliant. A good associate of mine has often observed, perhaps cynically, that networking can only mean one thing: 'the gathering of other hungry consultants'! If there were plenty of work queuing to be tackled, would there be such a strong need to network amongst similar minds? For some, networking can bring benefits of comradeship, some reassurance and the sharing of good quality knowledge/advice.

Many successful consultancies have relied on good partnerships of at least two persons. The main rationale hinges on the fact that you could pool resources (intellectual kind) together, to enhance the overall effectiveness of your practice. For some people, this is the only way they can work comfortably and well, since working alone is often unworkable for them. Others may prefer to operate independently and not having the obligation to consult frequently for consensus. Consultants, by their nature and imposed expectations, tend to have strong views most of the time. In fact, if they don't, they are unlikely to have good, solid, distinctive advice to give! To expect total harmony and consensus with everyone else all the time, is probably asking too much. This dilemma is fairly prevalent in most organisations offering professional services where some degree of in-fighting or power struggle exists.

Following on from the above, I have been a member of the Lamberhurst network of consultants – not a totally new concept. Thus, I was formally linked up with over 40 (at time of writing) independent consultants, whose skills and expertise could virtually cover every business and management facet. Theoretically, this meant that we could undertake bigger projects involving bigger clients and internally cross-refer projects, which might fall outside our own specialities. There are other potential benefits, which I will leave you to think of. Irrespective of the network's directors, there may be issues in such business arrangements. How good a networker are you? Is it easy to be 100% fair in operating such a network or to accept the inevitable inequity that can exist in practice? If you have to contribute financially to the central pot, is there any tangible gain promised? Are you happy to share your uniqueness

(USPs) and ideas with 'strangers'? How much 'take' (or net gain) are you allowed?

A similar situation occurred many years ago when I paid a handsome fee to join a consulting franchise based in Berkeley Square, London. It was an innovative business concept then, which attracted a sizeable number of 'consultants' as their investors. However, this set-up lasted only months before the directors' apparent incompetence and extreme greed caused the company to collapse eventually. However, I did learn fast enough to help compensate my own loss. Presumably, the main lesson learnt was that you have to evolve your own needs for a reliable support system. By nature, most consultants are fairly independent and radical in their approach and hence may not naturally make good team players. It is probably true too that only a minority is smarter and more successful than others. So, are you smart and fit enough to survive?

Selling and image

As far as direct, face-to-face selling is concerned, you should realise that not everyone is cut out to sell. Fortunately for the successful few, not everyone is endowed with the gift of the intelligent and convincing gab. But sales are essential for survival. If you are inclined to be introverted or shy in approaching strangers, many disappointments and frustrations can then be expected. You can certainly learn and polish up various behavioural techniques, and some improvements should be then be forthcoming. But if you are fundamentally unattracted to the selling process, it would be best to employ or pay someone else to fulfil this specific role and confine yourself to the 'doing' aspect. In many instances, there is only one chance or opportunity to maximise your initial impact with the prospect. Personally speaking, I have been fortunate and have survived well due to a very steep learning curve on the selling approach at the very early stages.

Being able to create the right impact initially and maintain it subsequently for as long as possible, are regarded as critical keys to success. In practice, it comes down to your behaviour, mannerisms, choice of words and subjects, accent, pitch and loudness of voice, dress sense and rapport building. Appearance is all-important too. Can you imagine a typical blue chip company director buying from a consultant who behaves and looks like a loud-mouthed market stall trader who is poorly groomed? Rather unlikely, you would think. Thus appropriate and acceptable grooming from head to foot should be reviewed. I doubt if driving a clapped-out banger or a brand new Rolls would make a positive impact either. Success breeds success, they say, and there is some element of truth in that. Would you be very happy to invest your hard-earned cash in someone who is apparently a failure and looks bad compared to you?

Relationships

As far as dealing with 'human' clients is concerned, there is a universal expectation for one to succeed in the relationship building area. Consulting is predominantly an activity comprising a high level of human interactions, i.e. where dealing with objects or machines is less important or predominant. This means high contact time, with maximum time spent with humans are to be expected. It is fairly well acknowledged that 'people will only buy from people they like', unless they are forced to do so. This can be a problem too If there is an element of discomfort with your client. Hence, this can mean quite a difficult demand on certain types of people to conform to naturally. Invariably, this can also mean that building long-term relationships must be an important strategy for ongoing, long-term success. I would return to my earlier comment on personal chemistry, which is rather pertinent here. Thus, it could be highly unrewarding to keep up the pretence of deriving real pleasure if you are dealing with someone you may happen to dislike intensely. This is the case for any length of time, let alone long term. So, if you naturally prefer to work without much human contact, it would be wise to be extra fastidious as to what type of consulting you would consider offering. In extreme cases, you might conclude that consulting is not for you at all.

The issue of relationships applies to many facets of your life as a consultant. Of great importance too, it also concerns relationships within the client organisation. You would naturally assume that the direct client (e.g. the immediate recipient of your services) is at the top of the list, then cascading down to virtually everyone else. Those occupying the PA and receptionist positions should also be given due consideration and importance. A 'good' word said by an internal 'gatekeeper' can help open an important 'gate' or two. There was the case of a factory director, whom I had inadvertently upset in one of my projects by asking my honest, probing questions about his style. This had probably resulted in him vetoing my offer of subsequent help to his company, even though the CEO would just simply call it 'poor presentation' on my part! You cannot definitely please 100% of the people! To me, it is often the dilemma of choosing between being happy or being right.

Other parties where relationships can play an important role are those who can offer you different types of support. Thus, these may be associates, other knowledge based suppliers or fellow consultants who can complement your offerings. These are the knowledge-laden people whose advice can help you tip the sales balance by providing invaluable insights. Obviously, nobody would know it all, hence my decision to link up with the Lamberhurst Network, hoping to secure leverage on these knowledge aspects.

Project execution

Beyond getting the order, the next stage of engagement normally involves fact finding or investigating. If you have an inquiring mind plus the natural urge to relentlessly seek the truth, then you should excel here. Not accepting what you are told initially and then asking the same question from more than one party within the client group can be useful. This helps to confirm and complete the various opinions offered.

You can be truly amazed by the range of possible answers – and varying degrees of passion attached too – in the answers given. Examples of this can be found in other sections of this book. The only main drawback on this is the minority, whom you might sometimes upset in the process. I refer here to those who are strongly egoistic and probably very proud, who might sense some threat to their own positions. Sometimes strong loyalty may emerge from a few who might feel that my presence is a threat to their bosses. They can therefore be rather unwilling or not readily open to accept, at least publicly, inaccuracies and misperceptions within their own judgements.

Having obtained the basic raw data, you would normally proceed onto the analysis phase. Being able to visualise the whole picture embellished with all the captured views, plus your own version and quite importantly, the context of the situation, can be a tough intellectual challenge. This is when your comprehensive (expected) experience and your partners' can be useful. This presupposes that your prejudices can be held in check with moderation. You could look for so-called patterns or themes which may become obvious in certain situations and cultures. For instance, a demoralised workforce might be caused by inequitable (perceived or real) management practices/policies, working environment (e.g. stresses), behaviours (e.g. conflicts), reward schemes, job satisfaction and/or prospects and promotion. This is the time when the right interpretations are key to offering realistic solutions, and not be led up the garden path or end up barking up the wrong trees!

Beyond analysis, the solutions stage will normally follow next. Normally, this forms the main area of interest for most clients. The success for this depends on your knowledge and conviction as to what could be the most practical and of the highest value to the client. A weaker consultant might be psychologically seduced to offer only the 'safe', low risk solutions, which would not always necessarily equate to being the 'best' in the client's interest. Is your preferred approach to say what your client wants to hear? It is again, really a case of 'horses for courses'. Mine tends to satisfy the criteria of being honest, pragmatic, feasible, innovative or proven, time and cost effective, and of general acceptability to the key players. Nothing beats your ability to draw upon the knowledge and experience from other similar, successful situations to help the current incumbents. One of my ex-teachers, Professor John Hunt of the London Business School once remarked that you should not kid yourself that we, as outsiders, would know the answers. According to him, the real solutions reside inside the client organisation. He might be right some of the time (in my opinion), and we should have the skills to tease that out. But you must never assume that the client in question knows any part of the answer. A consultant can certainly help him to develop it but it would be obvious naivety to expect clients to offer all the ideas or solutions without some effort from us. At the very least, our presence would suggest that we are needed to confirm the clients' suspicions. Ultimately, from an ethical standpoint, it is the consultant's responsibility to provide the best possible answer(s) and solutions.

Implementation

Writing reports is normally expected by most clients. Helping to implement your prescribed solutions via careful handholding is the ultimate service a consultant can offer. This is when the hardened men or consulting veterans and the boys (juniors) could go separate ways. This would be the point when the client could discover whether s/he had just paid for a paper exercise, rubber-stamping or ideally much more. To execute this part well, it requires your knowledge, experience and courage to overcome possibly quite severe internal resistance and objections. Objections may appear from any quarter but these should be regarded as normal, and should be accepted as such. There have been times when I have been facing a mountain of resistance, alone – a fairly daunting situation for anybody to be in. But with strong convictions and proven guiding principles, you should normally win the day or at least gain partial victory.

Personally, I prefer to feel guilt free and can therefore sleep well at night, every night!

Another facet in implementation lies with the client. Effective harnessing of their internal resources in the implementation phase always makes very good sense. Even a horde of life changing consultants would find it almost impossible to put into place all the agreed 'best practices', let alone by a single consultant. Achieving this successfully is a true test of the consultant's interpersonal/persuasive skills, competence and in depth knowledge of human behaviour. Good analyses and inferences normally form the solid basis to ensure success here.

Imagine the scenario in which the key people have just realised the mistakes they had themselves have made, their own shortcomings and that, worst of all, they now face the prospect of being shown up as incompetent in public (i.e. the bosses, peers, and subordinates)? This is the so called eureka moment that many seek. It requires a high confidence level and deep personal conviction to help steer the client away from their own garden path of near certain doom. This is the area where many consultants fail to deliver appropriately. To survive the omnipresent politics (thriving well in most organisations), the ability to handle conflicts well, being able to read the clients' minds, offer solid arguments (every time) against the main tide, maintain your professional composure and be infinitely patient are some of the key requirements. I reiterate that without a high level of professional commitment, resilience, interpersonal skills and insight, it would be quite tough to perform well at this stage.

By now, it should be obvious that to really succeed as a consultant is a major challenge which not everyone could undertake lightly and overcome. Certainly, there are handsome rewards to be reaped from executing an assignment satisfactorily. But the converse is possible and true, especially for the juniors in the profession.

Ultimately, it is a case of being honest (normally the best policy!) with yourself as regards your capability, to determine objectively the real probability of success, and it is also important to be realistic in accepting the conclusions. Hopefully, my main objective for sharing frankly some of my views with all of you has been achieved. The above ideas have been learnt the very hard, sometimes bruising and costly, way. But there have been periods when there was real fun and high levels of personal satisfaction. You might well be right in assuming that I have retained a few more tips up both my rather long sleeves!

Chapter 8   Do Consultants get Rewarded?

Having read through the negative and perhaps seemingly frustrating sections of this book, you may well be wondering if consultants ever end up receiving any sort of reward at all.

Positive rewards

The short answer to that in this short chapter (for sake of completeness) is a definite and resounding 'YES'. Despite the fact that I have deliberately moaned very freely about prospects and clients in earlier chapters, most successful consultants do get their due rewards. The latter would normally commensurate fairly well with the end results and achievements. If the rewards were absent, I doubt if consultancy could have become one of the most popular modern professions, especially amongst bright, young graduates. What follows can be described as what I would regard as 'rewards' in the broadest sense of the word.

To me, the greatest reward is the positive personal feeling and deep sense of satisfaction of having achieved the objective I have set out to achieve in the first place. This would be something well-defined with my client and agreed as my personal target. It would also be a kind of relief off my shoulders that the seemingly insurmountable (sometimes) challenge to be resolved, has finally been tackled. It actually boils down to being able to observe the resulting improvements and hear from those involved how things have improved for them, as compared to their recent, worse past.

It may sound surprising to my clients that, apart from being paid the monetary fee which is officially due, an important aspect to me (and most humans) comes from their 'glowing' compliments. The latter could come by way of verbal feedback in our interactions or from letters or referrals. In Transactional Analysis terms, that would be classified as positive psychological 'strokes'. However, in offering a service, I do not consciously seek out gratitude and appreciation. One can detect those when they are present. My chief aim is to execute my agreed task well.

One attraction of being a consultant must be the sense of belonging to the profession itself. It is certainly a privileged profession since several trade bodies have tried to dominate and control using the guise of accreditation, licensing or establishing professional standards. For those fellow veterans, we should regard ourselves as on par with the 'bosses' we serve, through our extensive knowledge, experience, objectivity and insights into their issues. This privileged position has helped us to get through the chaos that exists in most organisations and somehow emerge with excellent solutions. This would be impossible if you were operating from within a tight hierarchical slot in a restrictive, organisational pyramid. Personally, I am now enjoying the pinnacle of my career, as I have started from quite humble, family origins in far-flung Malaysia. My father was a clerk and eventually a typical Chinese businessman. Being predominantly self-trained (without being moulded by any established and strong consulting cultures) and now operating successfully as a professional adviser has given me an immense sense of satisfaction. As a teenager, I would never have predicted that this day would come, albeit four decades later. That is, I am now in an established position in which I am able to confidently advise the professional business group that I once greatly revered.

Another source of reward has come from my meetings with hundreds of interesting individuals, including my clients, colleagues and fellow 'competitors'. Some of these I have come to know fairly well. If this concerns my clients, I am then able to provide them with advice that could be said to penetrate beneath their 'skin' depths. There is also the intellectual reward associated with getting to know about various types of industries and cultures.

Most organisations have inner secrets which they would regard as sacrosanct facets or even shame, to be hidden at all costs from prying, external eyes. As an outsider, and initially, as a stranger, it can be a rather tall order to get to hear and be trusted with their innermost fears. Psychologically speaking, it is rather similar to donning the priest's clothes, listening to hair-raising confessions. To reach that level of trust and sometimes being given a share of the commercially sensitive/confidential information is indeed a heart warming achievement. Over the years, I have heard many amazing 'confessions' regarding a wide variety of situations.

As someone probably endowed with a 'good' incisive intellect, I have found most of my assignments to be intellectually stimulating. I have been handed many tough challenges, whereby my analytical and holistic (seeing all aspects of the situation) abilities have had to be flexibly deployed over the years. More importantly, I have been able to indulge myself in enjoying the priceless luxury of being able to learn new concepts, ideas, 'best' practices etc., which I can apply.

Your bonus

One extremely interesting outcome of this prolonged exposure to hundreds of people has been the opportunity for me to assimilate and appreciate the infinite variations of behaviours. These I have classified into certain patterns of personalities based on their dates of birth using an ancient (several thousand years old) but popular concept. This has been modified by proofs of correlations that I have collated over more than 25 years. But I must admit that the methodology employed is nowhere near as rigorous as that of an academic.

I have given below 36 different combinations of dates of births, accompanied by my predictions of their likely personality and behaviours. If you happen to have the same birth date or know of someone who does, then you are in luck and can enjoy this 'bonus' bit of personal information! The predictions will be less accurate if your year of birth is different. The characteristics given under each birth date are just a tiny selection from a longer list.

13 Jan 1970
Active   vocal   assertive

25 Jan 1947
Cultured   mild mannered   intellectual   political

4 Feb 1967
Philosophical   likes limelight   acting skill   political

9 Feb 1962
Assertive   leadership potential   scientific minded

23 Feb 1951
Aesthetic   diplomatic   creative   multitalented

27 Feb 1941
Extremely 'slippery'   intuitive   sensitive   political

14 Mar 1977
Sensitive   unpredictable   cowardly   devious

24 Mar 1975
Potential leadership material   researcher   thinker

10 Apr 1964
Domineering   hot/cold approach   extraverted   socially active

18 Apr 1953
Intuitive approach   possibly inconsistent   arts oriented

23 Apr 1955
Plodding nature   normally calm   generally sober   musical

27 Apr 1966
Average flexibility   scientific minded   mild mannered

5 May 1980
Practical   shrewd   moderately assertive

4 June 1971
Generally good natured   can converse   acting ability   artistic

9 June 1946
Ideas person   communicator   sporty writer

14 June 1969
Sharp tongued   communicator   very changeable   musical

27 June 1960
Business acumen   slick talker   musical

14 July 1949
Tenacious   imaginative   creative   changeable

15 July 1945
Cautious   critic   historian

26 July 1958
Good confidence   reasonably stable   slight rebellious streak

14 Aug 1960
Cliquey   some business acumen   some inflexibility

20 Aug 1952
Very proud   confident   fairly rigid outlook

4 Sept 1978
Probably a perfectionist   social orientation   physical

12 Sept 1968
Creative   diplomatic   intelligent

16 Sept 1959
Quietly critical   writer   diplomatic

30 Sept 1952
Balanced outlook   musical   judgemental

8 Oct 1949
Variable temperament   tactful   good action orientation

13 Oct 1984
Peaceable   writer   aesthetic   academic

5 Nov 1957
Tough outlook   sharp tongued   strong approach

13 Nov 1955
Strongly opinionated   administrator   sensitive   suspicious

17 Nov 1978
Even tempered   teacher   intellectual

5 December 1949
Reasonably easygoing   enjoys conversation   potentially an ideas person

9 Dec 1950
Very independent minded   good adviser   confident

9 Dec 1962
Generally pleasant   expressive   vocal talent

23 Dec 1956
Financially shrewd   crafty approach   leader   writer

28 Dec 1962
Pessimist   traditional   serious worker   thinker

The above should be seen as a tempting taster and there will
definitely be sceptics amongst you. The chief implication for
giving the above is that I am now able to predict fairly
accurately a stranger's basic personality even though I have

never met him in person. Obviously, this should be regarded as a guess, though a very good one at times, and as such, can never be 100% accurate. But, it can be a highly invaluable tool for me to use in prospecting for new business. Inevitably, it has also helped my clients to recruit key staff and also to better understand and prepare themselves for future interactions with these people. The good thing is that no one needs to spend time and money completing a psychometric personality instrument (happens to be one of my popular offerings). Better still, the target does not need to know that s/he has been analysed! That is, their permission is not necessarily required and there is no requirement for their personal or conscious involvement if they are not interested. For my part, it is a *fait accompli* too, since I am unconcerned as to whether my predictions are accepted or not. It is really a case of 'take it or leave it'.

Thus, I can, to a good degree, predict whether a person may possess any of the following main characteristics:

Risk averse	Careful	Moody	Personable	Impatient
Extravert	Introvert	Leadership	Inventive	Action oriented	Egoistic
Impulsive	Positive	Apprehensive	Enthusiastic	Stable	Inflexible
Stubborn	Kind	Methodical	Persevering	Peaceable
Flexible	Intellectual	Creative	Hands-on	Imaginative	Changeable
Expressive	Versatile	Communicative	Talkative	two-faced	Tenacious
Caring	Sympathetic	Sensitive	Patient	Proud	Generous
Confident	Peevish	Bossy	Loyal	Trusting	Critical
Crafty (physically skilled)	Diligent	Subservient	Selfish	Intelligent
Discriminating	Perfectionist	Flirtatious	Finely balanced
Non-confrontational	Restless	Judgemental	Objective	Friendly
Suspicious	Curious	Analytical	Team player	Independent	Opinionated
Vindictive	Open minded	Philosophical	Carefree
Mentor	Tense driven	Candid	Free spirited	Pessimist	Shrewd
Ambitious	Thrifty	Traditional	Reserved	Tactful	Truth seeker
Curious	Sociable	Rebellious	Perverse	Original	Detached
Altruistic	Inventive	Humane	Cool manner	Kind	Reforming

Helpful	Selfless	Indecisive	Devious	Charming	Empathetic
Intuitive	Protective	Pragmatic	Gentle	Resolute	Patient
Dependable	Dedicated	Unpredictable	Impulsive	Dynamic	Reckless
Articulate	Peaceable	Good counsel	Thorough	Astute	Inscrutable
Suave	Opportunistic	Dramatic	Dogmatic	Demanding	Decisive
Brash	Overconfident	Doer	Dutiful	'My Way'	Thinking
Ruthless	Possessive	Perceptive		Popular	Self-reliant
Nonconformist	Manipulative	Demanding		Persuasive	Problem solver
Sincere	Forgiving	Soft seller	Motivating	Competitive	Unsinkable
Calculating	Resourceful	Strategic	Warm	Decisive	
Abrasive	Aloof	Thorough	Watchful	Precise	Energetic
Honest	Straightforward	Reasonable		Quick tempered	Plain talking
Fearless	Outspoken	Erratic	Introverted	Logical	Quarrelsome
Insightful	Thoughtful	Naïve	Calm	Understanding	Selfless
Credible	Affable	Personable	Thick skinned	Obliging	Direct

There have been many projects where some emotional pain had existed. Each example of pain would have a threshold, beyond which my clients would find it rather difficult to endure. My intervention then would simply be just to help reduce or remove this pain. These have been real life dilemmas within situations where people's careers, livelihoods and egos had been involved. A few of these are now outlined to illustrate.

A few 'bosses' would naturally occupy top positions but they might somehow feel unsure of their own personal competences to discharge their responsibilities competently. This might be described as being aware of one's Achilles' spots. Others have indeed asked the question, 'How did these bosses get there in the first place?' Perceptive answers to that question would also provide possible clues on how to help them. Inevitably, being positioned at the apex of an organisation would mean having relatively few reassuring bodies on either side of a potentially lonely or isolated situation. Being asked to provide good, objective and all round perspectives into such spotlights can be gratifying. It can sometimes be a case of being candid to your client as to his suitability in handling that level of responsibility. The key lies in understanding his motivational needs, psychological makeup or innate personality, against the backdrop of his organisational circumstances. Obtaining the high level of trust is a prerequisite to being able to help him effectively.

As I am quite keen to understand and observe human behaviour and motivations, it is often quite fulfilling to be able to do that. This is especially true when I have come via a purely technical route and not a professional HR, psychological or psychiatric one. Thus, I have been able to make the multiple observations, analyse and finally convey my appropriate conclusions. As a bonus, I have often been instrumental in subsequent handholding and implementing the agreed outcomes. The latter can be fairly complex at times.

Negative rewards

It would be wrong of me not to point out the 'negative' rewards that might come your way as a consultant. By comparison, there are only a few of these and much has been written in the other chapters. In fairness, the positive rewards have far outweighed the negative ones. However, I would like to highlight a few of these negatives next for the sake of completeness.

First, I have met people I would term 'ungrateful' clients (also see Chapter 4). Although small in number by comparison, they seem to begrudge me for exposing their sacred cows within their organisations. You could argue that a key benefit of employing an outsider's expertise is to help identify work practices or cultural habits that have proved detrimental to the organisation's health. Exposing serious weaknesses can be shocking (to put it mildly?), but it could well be the essential lifeline that the organisation should actively seek to ensure its survival.

Then there are not clients, but prospects (probably better described as 'suspects'), who have really 'messed' me about in terms of what they have been hoping for, and have delayed communicating their decisions. One prime example related to a portable accommodation hire firm, based in the West which eventually changed ownership (an MBO). My phone calls were never returned despite the fact that the managing director had expressed and confirmed his interest in the review project for his several branch offices. Much effort was put in because he had changed his mind at least four times regarding the schedule! From analysing his birth date, I can now confirm that he belonged to the category of people where integrity, maturity and business ethics were sadly, somewhat lacking. I have now rightly decided to delete him from my contact list.

Similar situations relate to companies that keep postponing their decisions indefinitely. This protracted affair could take many months of communication, whilst waiting for the management concerned to have the guts to perhaps say, 'No, thank you'. I do wonder what they could have gained by their procrastination. The latter would have given them a negative telling off internally for not resolving their issues, apart from the fact that there might be some 'costs' incurred.

Another frustration, probably more for the prospect than the consultant, occurs when I have identified and could very clearly see the harmful symptoms within. You can easily argue that these are the prime candidates that should be offered help since they would definitely need help. Due to the personalities involved (with regard to some, birth date examples are given above) and negative internal opinions of using external advice, there have been difficulties convincing the suspect to decide on taking action. Ultimately, we understand that hard-earned cash is involved here but also ultimately, it could also mean the end of a company, and potentially associated losses to its stakeholders.

A relevant factor to be mentioned here concerned the perception of consultants in general by the business community. There will always be bad apples in any full barrel.

Thus, some consultants may well act without integrity, which is to be deplored if we regard ourselves as professionals.

The final point concerns the consultant's home life. As in most all-consuming (can certainly be!) *pre*occupations, consulting can take its toll emotionally and physically. This should not be surprising since commitment must be or expected to be total in order to ensure that one's best efforts are given. Hence, the consequences can wreak havoc, especially to your family life, which in normal circumstances, might have been regarded as relatively stable.

Consulting can be regarded as a fairly unique profession where no two assignments need be the same and are unlikely to be the same. This is probably the case since business situations often emerge from the outcome of complex interactions of environmental factors and human decisions. It definitely appeals to those with a strong preference for mental achievement, good affiliation with people and also a moderately strong power/ego need to influence or control others. Personally speaking, it is probably one of the most 'rewarding', job satisfaction wise, professions anyone could ever have.

Chapter 9   Conclusions on Clients – *Caveat Consultants!*

In my view, business management consulting hovers at or near the top of all the intellectually challenging professions. To succeed well in it is no mean feat. Many people have come in for a fast taster ranging from weeks to a year or so and have then left the consulting arena for good. Others have comfortably latched onto the 'big boys' for a ride during a honeymoon period in the 'up or out' culture, possibly followed by something akin to a roller coaster journey. Many have had it fairly easy, possibly by indulging in the 'licking of someone's tasty boots' or attaching themselves to governmental, quasi business bodies or biggish networks. The rest, veterans such as I, who have literally started from scratch at ground level, are very few and far between because many would not have earned enough to survive. According to one Chinese saying, 'The older brain is wiser and the older devil is more accurate'. Hence, clients should naturally gravitate towards the older members of our profession.

'Borrow *your* watch to tell *my* time'

In my many journeys and conversations, I have heard negative comments made about consultants. The most known one is 'they borrow your watch to tell the time'. There is, without any doubt, some element of truth in that. As one also hears, 'there's no smoke without fire'. I have heard many stories of consultants who were paid to produce reports, which would disappointingly contain mainly publicly-known, i.e. stale, information and rubber-stamping. In response, I will say that every client is different because of their history, culture, leadership, customers, staff, products, markets etc, etc. To be effective, a consultant needs to learn enough to ensure that his offer is the 'best' possible advice to suit that situation. Inevitably, as part of the influencing process, the end must include selected information (as solid evidence), which is probably well known to the client. It is impossible to provide effective help if their needs are unknown and not well understood. My best response to that remark is, 'Yes, I may borrow your watch if I don't already have one, but it will be returned to you in a far better state'. I would also add, 'The refurbished state of your watch should also give you superior accuracy, amongst other benefits, thus far outweighing the fair investment you might have made.'

This book was written to provide good, basic realism, sprinkled with a modicum of humour and home truths about the types of people that make up the client or prospect population. Most of my clients are normal, sensible and intelligent (though not necessarily of MENSA calibre) human beings. Strange enough, I did help a fellow MENSAN with his gold and silver-plating business with pleasant results. The rest, i.e. the other minority, including prospects, can be somewhat quirky, testing or frustrating. To put it bluntly, some would definitely be put in the not 'thin' (intellectually speaking, but the th--k) category.

As a well-seasoned consultant who has been in contact with thousands, I am happy to share my final thoughts with you about the all-important topic of:

Clients or Prospects (Who/What are they?)

They –

- Are, first and foremost, called clients because they must have an identifiable, urgent need or several needs that need to be resolved. The latter can mean a complex situation of someone with serious problems. If there is no definable need, whether it be real or perceived, there will be no solid basis of a business relationship with a consultant.

- May only seek help as a last resort, probably after ALL else have apparently failed.

- May not know what their real needs are. But we are here to help, aren't we? Do they know what we can help them with...and how? It is the consultant's real duty to explain and convince, i.e. sell and sell! This may only be possible if there is sufficient 'chemistry' to mutually lock both parties in. The 'bonus' in Chapter 8 may provide a clue or answer.

- Can be confused as to what they *want*, rather than what they actually *need*; hence quite susceptible to the really persuasive.

- Some of them (due to their own intransigence) are best left alone to stew or wallow in their own ill-fated destiny (of bankruptcy, liquidation, takeover or insolvency, illness, stress, redundancy).

- Can make excellent lifelong friends but beware of how you would decide to mix the business with the pleasure (if there is any) and still maintain your effectiveness and objectivity.

- Cannot be expected to open their hearts fully when you first meet them, unless your approach is flawlessly superb and all convincing. Almost inevitably, there is a courting period as this is expected in most newish type relationships.

- May well surprise you by lending you their proverbial organisational watch(es) for you to tell them the exact or better time. Their owners are probably too visually impaired or even blinkered to trust themselves. But do not be fooled; can you really read their watches and offer them an accurate time? What do you have that they don't?

- May sometimes borrow *your* watch (for free and indefinitely) so that they themselves will know the time, obviously for *gratis*!

- May expect kindness, integrity, patience, effectiveness, honesty and leadership from you and even be occasionally flavoured with a dollop of subservience. Is this acceptable to you?

- May agree to meet you purely out of plain curiosity and courtesy (especially the ones who can't say 'No'). This will usually lead to nothing financially and be just added to your colourful tapestry of life experiences.

- May also initially agree to meet you but can quickly change their minds, as other apparently 'more' important circumstances emerge or their fancies have gone elsewhere.

- May have this attitude of expecting advice or help for nothing, sometimes.

- May not pay you in full, even if the work has been completed satisfactorily to mutually agreed terms.

- Can be a real, annoying nuisance or even be justifiably labelled as SOBS or BA*T**DS (as an associate has so justifiably put). They can also be really fickle.

- Are an interesting, sometimes enigmatic breed, which even this book cannot do them full injustice.

- If they are tiny organisations (i.e. the micro businesses with limited funds), they should normally be best left alone as the pitiful untouchables, unless for altruistic reasons.

- Should really be made aware of the precious time they can waste and have wasted in this world. This applies to many of those at the lower echelons (including directors) of organisations who don't have the minimal budget or necessary authority to decide.

- May treat consultants as non-humans ('dirt'?) by not reciprocating with the standard, expected courtesy, mutual respect (sometimes not in their vocabulary) etc.

- May have something to hide (e.g. their imminent fate or secretive circumstances?) and will never tell you the full story – possibly to mutual detriment.

- May decide to wither off into oblivion rather than ingest their ego/pride by accepting your help.

- May possibly, have got the timing wrong in not calling you to come back earlier and is now a dead statistic.

- Can sometimes be persuaded to part with huge sums by those 'big boys' in the business and can still feel relatively happy about it. It is a case of who pays the money and can thus take the choice. Sadly, sometimes the 'smaller boys' can produce equivalent or better results for infinitely much less dosh! Perhaps it is 'easy come, easy go'.

- Can be used as an effective marketing tool for you if they are willing and after they themselves have enjoyed the benefits, i.e. having been suitably impressed by your efforts.

- May only be a client once, when they did have a problem or more. So don't expect past clients to remain as your active clients indefinitely.

My professional life has had a fair share of ups and downs, e.g. the oft-mentioned feast and famine syndrome. In pursuit of business deals, I have met thousands of people over the years. Without a doubt, it has been interesting, mentally challenging and sometimes terribly frustrating. The last refers mainly to situations where I could see real, very serious issues, which require pragmatic actions then, not weeks or months later. But, apparently, the prospect did not share my concerns for them, and inevitably, a few of them did vanish from the business world.

In my opinion, donning the sales hat and keeping it on for extended periods is the most challenging/demanding stage of any consulting cycle. This means adopting the appropriate positive persona and metamorphosing (temporarily) oneself into one with a fairly thick psychological skin. Rejections of your services can come thick and fast, sometimes for months in a row despite good qualifications of the prospects' circumstances to increase the probability of success. Sad to say, this has happened on and off, over the years. These zero payoffs are often the major cause of consultants throwing in the proverbial towel, even on a perfectly sunny, English summer's day.

Those of you who are contemplating a similar career will now have in your hands much of the information needed to make your own 'best' decision. In a way, it can be an interesting alternative to labouring as someone else's subordinate in a corporate world. There are bosses and bosses and probably they would make a good subject for another story.

But, do you personally have the essential personality traits of tenacity, keen observation and analysis, supported by a caring enough nature to succeed? These traits are important even if you may currently lack the much valued experience and expertise. Even if you are truly a unique expert (no such animal?), can you influence and sell yourself effectively and establish a sustainable reputation from your efforts? These are the key questions for all budding consultants to answer.

Without problems there would be no clients. Without 'good' clients, there will be no consultants, i.e. we will not exist. Not all consultants are bad, so to speak. Some consultants are acceptable or mediocre and a small minority can even be excellent. There are good clients too – those who will tell all, ideally ASAP to save time, whatever they think they can...and of course, they must pay their dues on time! Common sense dictates that there will always be a need for the high quality, honest, effective and committed consultant. However, in real consulting, both prospects and clients may not take kindly to the junior consultant, possibly one lacking grey hairs......yet! It takes more than pure guts to advise someone who might be 30 years or more senior in age.

Logically, my final words must be dedicated to my own appreciative clients. To them, I say thank you for giving me the pleasure by doing business with K-L Associates of Harrow. More importantly, I am particularly grateful to those who have been open, frank and ethical in their dealings with me and my associates. To those individuals, including prospects, who have been less than frank or somewhat devious, it is regrettable that we have irretrievably lost both our time and efforts. As life is short, our new awareness should encourage us to interact more fruitfully next time. That is, if indeed there *is* a next time for us to meet again!

Happy consulting, everyone! Or, hopefully, be effectively consulted?

'Real Solutions Come From Whole Truths'

Printed in the United Kingdom
by Lightning Source UK Ltd.
135908UK00001B/120/P